Wantagh Public Library

3 4873 00405 2866

W9-BWN-112

978.032
O

Olsen, Russell A.,
1954-

Route 66, lost &
found.

31.95

DATE			

WANTAGH PUBLIC LIBRARY
3285 PARK AVENUE
WANTAGH, NY 11793
(516) 221-1200
03/08/2006

BAKER & TAYLOR

ROUTE 66
LOST & FOUND

RUINS AND RELICS REVISITED

RUSSELL A. OLSEN

MBI

DEDICATION

This book is dedicated to my mother and father,
Russell and Catherine, and to all the
dedicated people involved in the preservation of
our nation's historic highways.

First published in 2004 by MBI Publishing Company, Galtier Plaza, Suite 200, 380 Jackson Street, St. Paul, MN 55101-3885 USA

© Russell A. Olsen, 2004

All rights reserved. With the exception of quoting brief passages for the purposes of review, no part of this publication may be reproduced without prior written permission from the Publisher.

The information in this book is true and complete to the best of our knowledge. All recommendations are made without any guarantee on the part of the author or Publisher, who also disclaim any liability incurred in connection with the use of this data or specific details.

We recognize that some words, model names, and designations, for example, mentioned herein are the property of the trademark holder. We use them for identification purposes only. This is not an official publication.

MBI Publishing Company titles are also available at discounts in bulk quantity for industrial or sales-promotional use. For details write to Special Sales Manager at Motorbooks International Wholesalers & Distributors, Galtier Plaza, Suite 200, 380 Jackson Street, St. Paul, MN 55101-3885 USA

ISBN: 0-7603-1854-9

Front Cover: Painted Desert Trading Post, Navajo, Arizona, c. 1942 (top) and 2003 (bottom)

Title Page: In 1947, author Russell Olsen's grandmother, cousin, and aunt (left to right) posed for this photograph along Route 66 in Lupton, Arizona. Olsen's grandfather, whose shadow is visible at the bottom of the frame, was the photographer.

Front Endpaper: Gascozark Café and Gas Station, Gascozark, Missouri, c. 1939

Rear Endpaper: Gascozark Café and Gas Station, Gascozark, Missouri, 2003

Back Cover: Meteor Crater Observatory, west of Winslow, Arizona, c. 1946 and 2003

3 4873 00405 2866

Edited by Dennis Pernu
Designed by Tom Heffron

Printed in Hong Kong

CONTENTS

PREFACE AND ACKNOWLEDGMENTS

In late summer 1995, I drove to Chicago from Los Angeles to visit my brother and his family. While there, I had the thought to drive Route 66 back west. I had always wanted to take this trip, and it seemed like the perfect opportunity to cross one of the items off my "things to accomplish in my life" list. So I borrowed a camera from my brother and bought a couple rolls of film on which to record my much-anticipated trip. I soon realized that two rolls of film were not going to cut it. I found a wealth of subject matter and wound up shooting 27 rolls of film on that trip.

That was the beginning of my fascination with America's Main Street. During the next few years I made the trip from Los Angeles to Chicago on an annual basis, spending most of my time photographing the many classic motels, cafés, and service stations along the route. I bought every book about Route 66 that I could get my hands on and read everything available on the history of the road. Around 1998, when I began collecting postcards of the route, it occurred to me that many of the places depicted on the postcards were either long gone or in danger of becoming lost to fast-food establishments, self-storage businesses, and mini malls. I began to get the idea of traveling to the sites pictured on the postcards and photographing them. As the project grew, I realized that it was important to record as many of these sites as possible before they were forever lost in the name of "progress." Future generations that might never have a chance to experience the Mother Road could look back and re-live a Route 66 road trip, if only in the pages of a book. The only problem was finding all of the vintage postcards I would need to make the project work.

I contacted collectors around the country and, to my surprise, all were willing to loan me their cards. In cases where postcards were not available of sites that I wanted to include in this book, I spoke with the owners of the properties and tried to acquire archival photos of these landmarks. I would like to thank the following people who allowed me access to their personal collections: Marion Clark, Earl and the late Cheryl Cory, Laurel Kane, Jeff Meyer, Steven Rider, Jim Ross, Mike Ward, and a very special thanks to Joe Sonderman. Without their help, this book could not have been made. I would also like to thank Brett Bather for all his encouragement during the making of this book.

After a year of gathering the cards and photos it was time to decide which sites I would use. It was a difficult task—all of them are important pieces of history that deserve to be cataloged. I had about 400 subjects to choose from, but had to narrow it down to 75 to fit the publisher's requirements. After the editing process, it was time to hit the road. The actual photography took place in June and July 2003. I began early one morning in Ludlow, California, but toward the end of the day experienced camera malfunctions and ended up spending a couple of days in a Kingman, Arizona, motel room while my camera was repaired back in Los Angeles. On the third day, after photographing the Meteorite Museum in Arizona, I experienced car problems and needed a tow to Holbrook. Unfortunately, it was a Saturday morning, and although it was only a minor radiator hose problem, all of Holbrook's garages were closed for the weekend. Again, I found a motel and sat around until Monday, when I found a mechanic. After a few hours I was again on my way. The rest of the trip went fairly smoothly, without any major problems.

The original idea was to take each shot from the exact spot that the postcard or archival photo was taken from. After the first day of shooting, however, I realized that that was not going to be possible. In many cases, the road had been widened, and standing in the middle of the road to shoot the photo was not an option. I also found that many of the buildings that I had planned to shoot had been expanded, or that trees had grown in, making the same angles virtually impossible. A few shots had to be altered simply because a freeway was built on top of the site where the photographer had taken the original postcard photograph. Every site I photographed presented its own unique problem. For perspective, look for small clues on the buildings like window patterns and backgrounds.

Also, as you read the book and go from state to state, imagine the many challenges that confronted early motorists who traveled Route 66. Imagine praying it does not rain while you're driving the treacherous Jericho Gap in Texas. Imagine worrying how far it is to the next service station because your gas gauge reads "E" and all that can be seen ahead is the black expanse of the nighttime desert. Traveling during the early days of motoring was an adventure. The places represented in this book were but a few of the many on Route 66 that fulfilled various needs for tourists and for travelers. I sincerely hope that some sense of that history and adventure comes through in the words and photographs presented in this book.

INTRODUCTION

U.S. HIGHWAY 66: AMERICA'S MAIN STREET

America has always been a nation of people on the go. While the methods of transportation have changed over the years, the goal remains.

Route 66 has its roots in the nation's old wagon trails. In 1857 Congress commissioned Lieutenant Edward Fitzgerald Beale to survey the land along the 35th Parallel from Fort Defiance near the New Mexico–Arizona border to the Colorado River. This route became known as Beale's Wagon Road, establishing a vital communication link to the West and serving as a military transport highway. Beale's Wagon Road, the Pontiac Trail in Illinois, the Ozark Trail in Missouri, and the old Santa Fe Trail were all in some form predecessors of what would become America's Main Street.

The turn of the twentieth century brought the burgeoning popularity of the automobile. Early automobile roads were primarily converted wagon trails and poorly marked, or not marked at all. As more and more people began using automobiles it became obvious that newer and better roads were needed. Grassroots "good road"

organizations and associations began popping up all over the country with the intent of improving roads and marking and mapping them.

By the mid-1920s about 250 marked trails existed across the country, all sponsored by local trail organizations. Since there wasn't a central organization coordinating these efforts, each association marked their trails in their own way. Some used painted stripes on fence posts, while others used symbols like the Indian head that guided folks along the Pontiac Trail in Illinois. These somewhat random and often overlapping markings created nightmares for early travelers. In 1924 the secretary of agriculture selected a board of state and federal highway officials to standardize a national highway numbering system and to explore the existing trails for possible use as part of a national highway system. Cyrus Avery, a state highway commissioner in Oklahoma, was among the officials selected to sit on the American Association of State Highway Officials. He worked with the chief engineer from Illinois, Frank Sheets, and chief engineer from Missouri, B. H. Piepmeier, on a proposed highway from Chicago to

Los Angeles. The proposed project was met with strong opposition because it was not considered a "tourist" route. (The fact that Avery routed the highway through his hometown didn't help matters.) Nevertheless, Avery and his associates believed strongly that this highway would become one of the country's most important highways. "There is more travel between Los Angeles and Chicago, or in that vicinity, than any other transcontinental route," Piepmeier wrote to Avery.

When it came time to number the road, the board chose 60 because all of the system's primary roads being planned were designated with numbers ending in zero. Officials in charge of the route from Virginia Beach to Springfield, Missouri, however, were also hoping to use that number and put up a fight to have their highway designated U.S. Highway 60. The disagreement continued for months until Avery and his associates eventually settled on the number 66 at the urging of Thomas H. MacDonald, chief of the Bureau of Public Roads, who was tired of the bickering. In November 1926, after two years of diligent work, the highway design and numbering system developed by Cyrus Avery and his associates was approved and set into motion.

Highway 66 followed a nontraditional diagonal path across Illinois, Missouri, Kansas, Oklahoma, Texas, New Mexico, Arizona, and California. The early route was made up of existing roads that zigzagged along county lines from town to town and state to state.

Individual states were for the most part responsible for road improvements and repairs from 1926 until 1933. In 1929 Highway 66 was fully paved in Illinois and Kansas. Missouri had 66 percent paved road and in Oklahoma 25 percent of the highway was hard road. In the western states early U.S. Highway 66 remained a primitive dirt byway with the exception of stretches in California's larger cities. Of 66's 1,200 miles west of Oklahoma, only 64.1 miles were paved.

By 1933 the federal government was taking an increased interest in the National Highway System, and President Franklin Roosevelt's New Deal program played a major role in the improvement of the nation's highways. From 1933 to 1938 the WPA (Works Progress Administration) and the CCC (Civilian Conservation Corps) worked to improve and maintain the National Highway System. By late 1937 the entire length of U.S. Highway 66 from Chicago to Los Angeles was paved.

With the country suffering economic depression, Midwestern farmers were hit with another disaster. A severe lack of rain coupled with strong winds turned farms in Oklahoma, Kansas, and Arkansas into a wasteland. An estimated 210,000 people left their homes behind during the so-called Dust Bowl and headed to California in search of a better life. Highway 66 became a road of flight and the path of choice for most of these farm families. John Steinbeck's 1939 novel *The Grapes of Wrath* immortalized the Dust Bowlers, forever linking them with Highway 66 and declaring the highway "The Mother Road."

During World War II Route 66 served as a main artery for military transportation and several installations were set up along or near Route 66. Between 1941 and 1943 more than 50 percent of all defense-related material needed for America's war production was transported and delivered by truck. At the onset of the war the government invested heavily in projects throughout California, primarily in the Los Angeles and San Diego areas. By 1943 a half million men and women were needed to meet production demands created by the war. With California's workforce depleted, people from outside the state filled most of these jobs. This new workforce traveled to California and new lives via Highway 66.

After World War II and the demise of gas and tire rationing, automobile travel exploded and the nation's busiest east-to-west highway overflowed. Hundreds of motels, cafés, and service stations sprang up along the entire route, ready to serve the increasingly mobile public. But the sudden influx of tourist travel and the lingering effects of heavy truck traffic during World War II took their toll on the road. By the early 1950s most of Highway 66 was too narrow to handle modern trucks and automobiles and was fast becoming obsolete. In 1956 the Federal Aid Highway Act was passed to provide expanded funding for the National Highway System, marking the end for America's Main Street. Newer four-lane roads built to Interstate standards began to open as early as 1958, and continued as rural areas were improved first, followed by town bypasses. As construction neared each small village and town many business owners who ran roadside tourist services simply closed their doors in anticipation of the worst. Some stayed, however, and saw traffic through their respective towns slow to a trickle.

Business owners along the route usually remember the exact time of day the Interstate opened around their towns. Most compare the experience to the closing of a water faucet. One day hundreds of cars passed in front of their businesses; the next day a dozen or so might pass. Businesses struggled, but most eventually failed, and by the late 1970s most of the route had been replaced. On October 13, 1984, Williams, Arizona, became the last town along Route 66 to succumb, and in 1985 the fabled U.S. Highway 66 was officially decommissioned and all remaining signage removed.

For close to 50 years Route 66 was the caretaker of dreams for thousands of people. It took five Interstates to replace Route 66: Interstate 55 from Chicago to St. Louis, Interstate 44 from St. Louis to Oklahoma City, Interstate 40 from Oklahoma City to Barstow, Interstate 15 from Barstow to San Bernardino, and Interstate 10 from San Bernardino to Santa Monica. Maybe one day a hundred years from now people will look at the Interstates with this same feeling of nostalgia and wonder, as their tireless hovercraft speed over obsolete roads and diners serve their favorite food via plastic tubes. Until that day arrives, take a page from songwriter Bobby Troup, circa 1946: "If you ever plan to motor west/Travel my way, take the highway that's the best."

ILLINOIS

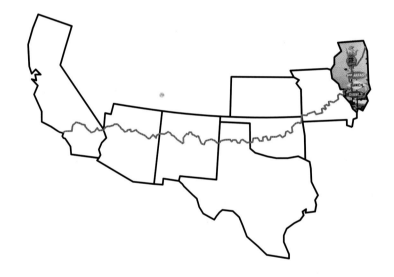

At the turn of the century roads and highways in the state of Illinois were primitive at best and impossible to navigate at worst. The history and development of Route 66 in Illinois can be traced back to these primitive roads and trails. In 1915 the main artery between Chicago and St. Louis was known as the Pontiac Trail, named for the eighteenth century chief of the Ottawa tribe. The trail was officially marked that same year with mile-by-mile guideposts from Chicago to St. Louis (courtesy of the B. F. Goodrich Company) ensuring even the novice traveler of at least having a chance of arriving at the proper destination. In 1918 a bond issue was passed for construction of hard roads in Illinois. The Pontiac Trail was designated SBI 4 (State Bond Issue) and began at 48th and Ogden in the western Chicago suburb of Cicero. After years of politicking and bureaucratic red tape, most of the road was finally paved by 1924, and by 1926 it was entirely a "hard road." The American Association of State Highway Officials approved the road for a U.S. Route designation and in 1927 U.S. Highway 66 signs were posted along its entire length.

Over the years many major changes took place to the routing of Route 66 in Illinois. In 1933 the easternmost terminus was moved from Cicero farther east to the entrance of Grant Park at Jackson Boulevard in Chicago. Another change took place in 1955 when Jackson became a one-way street and the official starting point was moved one block north to Adams Street, making the official endpoint the intersection of Jackson and Lake Shore Drive. In 1931 the original routing that followed Illinois Route 4 from Springfield to Staunton was rerouted to the east from Springfield to Litchfield, continuing to Mt. Olive. Another realignment occurred in the early 1930s when the route through Joliet and Wilmington was changed to alternate status and primary Highway 66 was redirected through Plainfield then on to Gardner, where the two versions of the route merged. As commercial truck traffic swelled and automobile traffic exploded throughout the late 1940s and into the 1950s, two-lane 66 was constantly improved and updated, and by 1957 the route was by and large a four-lane highway. The added improvements helped solve the congestion and safety problems but were no cure; it became painfully evident that Route 66 was outdated. It was the beginning of the end of the Mother Road in Illinois. By the mid-1970s most of Route 66 had been replaced with the new and modern Interstate 55. On January 17, 1977, the Illinois Department of Transportation removed the signs from the easternmost terminus, marking the official end of Route 66 in Illinois.

Today's traveler can still find much of the charm of old Route 66 in Illinois as they drive south from the towering concrete caverns of downtown Chicago, to the suburbs of Cicero and La Grange, and on through plains towns like Godley, Gardner, Dwight, Odell, Cayuga, Pontiac, Chenoa, Towanda, Funks Grove, Atlanta, Broadwell, Glenarm, Farmersville, Litchfield, Hamel, and Mitchell. To some, these small communities may be little more than dots on a map, but make no mistake: every town, motel, service station, mechanic, café, waitress, and short-order cook along the highway played an important role in shaping the history of Route 66 in Illinois.

WISHING WELL MOTEL, LA GRANGE
c. 1946

The Wishing Well Motel was built by John Blackburn in 1941 at the corner of Route 66 (now Joliet Road) and Brainard Avenue, just 15 miles from the heart of downtown Chicago. When built, the motel consisted of 10 cabins, an office, and a small house out back. Blackburn later sold the property to the Bronsons, who in turn sold it to Emil and Zora Vidas in 1958. In 1960 the individual cabins were connected to increase capacity, and in 1983 the property underwent more remodeling with the addition of four units. The small house in back was also converted to guest quarters, upping the room count to 19. In 1985 Zoras's husband Emil passed away and Zora has been manager and caretaker ever since.

For 62 years the Wishing Well has treated its guests to a quiet, country-like atmosphere just out of shouting range of the big city. In the early 1960s the nearby Willowbrook Ballroom booked swing and dance bands for months at a time and the Wishing Well became a home away from home for the musicians. Members of the rock band Chicago were also guests in the early 1970s, although Zora was admittedly quite hesitant about renting to "those kids with that long hair." Through its many renovations and improvements, the Wishing Well has managed to keep its charm, and it still readily serves weary travelers each night. And, yes, there is an above-ground stone well on the premises.

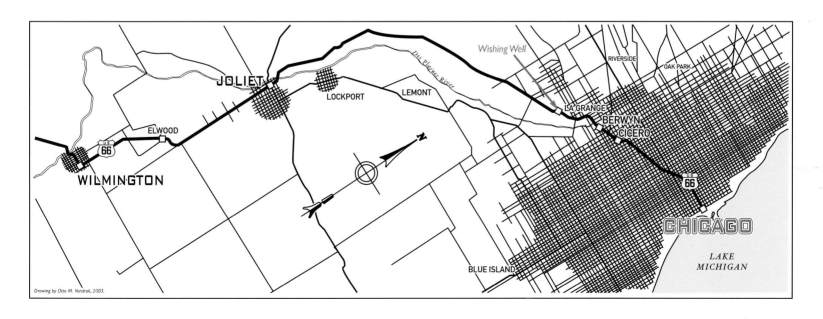

Drawing by Otto M. Vondrak, 2003.

THE RIVIERA, GARDNER
c. 1946

Established in 1928 by James Girot, a businessman from nearby South Wilmington, the Riviera Restaurant and Tavern is located on Route 66 (now Route 53) 60 miles south of Chicago. Buildings from the towns of Gardner (a church) and South Wilmington (a coal mine office) were moved and combined on-site to form the Riviera, which during its heyday also featured a zoo, picnic grounds, and a swimming hole, with the picturesque Mazon River just a couple of yards away. At the height of its popularity, the Rivera's restaurant was located upstairs, serving homemade Italian food, chicken, steak, and seafood. The lower portion of the building was a tavern.

The Riviera is rich in Route 66 history and Chicago gangster lore.

Al Capone and his brother Ralph often wet their whistles in the downstairs speakeasy after checking on their stills in nearby Kankakee County. Gene Kelly was also a frequent customer. In 1933 a gasoline station was added but was eventually shut down. In 1972 Bob and Peggy Kraft purchased the Riviera from the Girots and have carried on the Riviera tradition of good food and drink. The restaurant and tavern are now both downstairs. The food is transferred from the upstairs kitchen via a dumbwaiter. Walking into the now-combined restaurant and tavern, visitors are instantly transported to another time when flappers and jazz music were the rage and the speakeasy was the place to get a drink and socialize with friends.

LOG CABIN INN, PONTIAC
c. 1939

On the north side of the onetime coal-mining town of Pontiac, Illinois, sits the venerable Log Cabin Inn, a restaurant built by Joe and Victor Selotti in 1926 of cedar telephone poles. The Log Cabin, which seats 45 diners, has changed little since this part of the highway was the main thoroughfare between Chicago and St. Louis. The interior walls are made of knotty pine, projecting the feel of an old time café—the cars outside provide the only clues this is not 1939. The Log Cabin Inn was once best known for its beef, barbecued over open charcoal; Joe did the barbecuing in a separate building with windows that allowed customers to watch.

The path of Route 66 originally ran on the eastern side of the restaurant next to the railroad tracks. When the road was realigned to the western side, the building was raised and rotated with horses so the front door once again faced the road. It was quite an event that brought out half the town to watch. Other than turning the building around, the only major change to the restaurant over the years was the addition of a front entry in 1990. Gina Manker, a waitress who has worked at the Log Cabin Inn on and off for 30 years, says her favorite time to work is in the very early morning when the farmers come in for their coffee. When asked why, she blushes and says, "Oh my, the things you hear!"

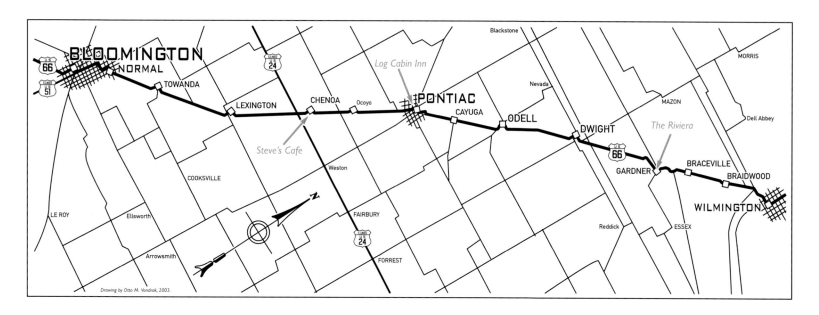

STEVE'S CAFÉ, CHENOA
c. 1950

The building that eventually housed Steve's Café was built in 1918 and was originally called Wahls Brothers. Steve's Café came about in the 1930s when new owner Steve Wilcox took over. People in the area still speak in reverence when referring to the pie and coffee served at Steve's. A Texaco service station was later added to the business. A canopy was added and the station was fully enclosed in the early 1970s. The Texaco station closed shortly thereafter and around 1975 that section of the building was turned into a bar called the Red Bird Lounge, named for the local Chenoa Red Birds high school sports teams. In 1975 Ken and Peg Sipe took over the building and continued to serve home-cooked meals and "World Famous Pie." During the summers, Steve's Café sponsored Friday-night fish fries at the local park. Peggy desperately tried to keep the café open after her husband was killed in an auto accident but eventually had to close the doors in 1997 after 22 years in business. Since the café's closure it has seen service as a used-car lot and an antique shop. Les Stevens, a Chenoa police officer, says what he remembers most about Steve's was the "huge steak-and-eggs breakfast with potatoes and the works for $3.99." The old cafe currently sits quietly on old 66, clinging to its past and hoping for a future.

"The Finest Steaks Between Chicago and St. Louis"
STEVE'S CAFE INTERSECTION CITY 66 & 24 CHENOA, ILLINOIS

DIXIE TRUCKERS HOME, McLEAN
c. LATE 1940s

J. P. Walters and his son-in-law, John Geske, built the Dixie Truckers Home in 1928 at the intersection of U.S. Routes 66 and 138 in McLean, Illinois. Housed in a rented garage, the first incarnation of the café had only a counter and six stools. Throughout its history, the Dixie Truckers Home has been constantly improved and remodeled. In the late 1930s six tourist cabins were added and eventually the café was expanded to serve 60 people. In 1965 a grease fire in the kitchen, aided by wooden exhaust ducts, destroyed the café. Amazingly, the tourist cabins and gas pumps were unscathed. In fact, that very evening, the gas pumps were back in business and one of the cabins was pressed into service as a temporary home for the café. The new Dixie Truckers Home reopened two years later with the capacity to serve 250 hungry travelers. The Dixie Truckers Home was not only consistently ranked among the nation's top 10 truck stops, serving customers with that southern hospitality its name implied, it was also home to the Route 66 Hall of Fame and Museum. At the time of this writing, the longtime family-owned truck stop was sold to a company based in Providence, Rhode Island, which planned to change the Dixie's name to Dixie Travel Plaza.

REDWOOD MOTEL, LINCOLN
c. 1965

Construction of the Redwood Motel began in 1955 and its first guests were welcomed in 1956. Built by Wilfred and Dorothy Werth, the Redwood sat conveniently at the junction of Routes 66, 10, and 21, with 15 rooms and a small living quarters attached to the main building. The exterior of the motel was originally constructed of stone and redwood, but by 1960 so many stones were falling off the walls that Wilfred decided to brick the entire exterior. The cost to stay at the Redwood in 1956 was $5 for a single and $8 for a double. When television was installed the rates were raised to $6 and $10, respectively.

In 1934, 22 years prior to opening the motel, Wilfred had built a Standard Oil station on the same corner. Wilfred proudly states that he had the "first gasoline pumps in the state that showed the dollars and cents through the small windows on the pumps." Wilfred, who turned 87 in 2003, adds that he and Dorothy "had fun" owning the motel but sold it in 1963 when Ruth Buckles made an offer he couldn't refuse. The station was sold in 1991 and is today a Quick Lube. The original motel sign was torn down after high winds ripped off a few letters, says current lessee Sherman West, and was replaced with a new sign in November 2002. Sherman and wife Joan have plans to renovate the entire motel, hoping to make it a "must" stop for travelers on Old 66.

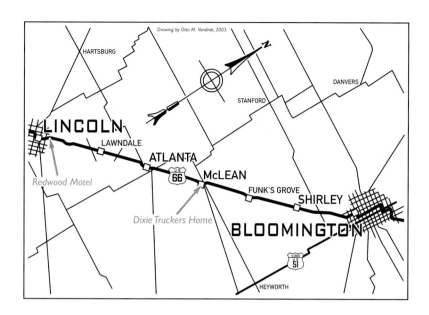

Drawing by Otto M. Vondrak, 2003.

ERNIE'S PIG HIP, BROADWELL
c. 1972

Ernie Edwards opened what would become the famous Pig Hip Restaurant in 1937 with three tables, a bar, $150 of borrowed money, and a desire to be his own boss. At first the restaurant was called the Harbor Inn because of a great deal Ernie found on wallpaper and restaurant glasses with a nautical theme. The name was shortlived. One day a hungry farmer came into the restaurant and spied a freshly baked ham on the stove. He pointed to the ham and said, "Give me a slice o' that pig hip." The rest, as they say, is history. Ernie applied for a patent on his sandwich (a generous helping of thinly sliced ham smothered with Pig Hip sauce) and copyrighted the name Pig Hip.

The sandwich was so popular that he opened two more restaurants in nearby towns but eventually closed them when he realized that managing two more Pig Hips was more than he had bargained for.

Ernie finally hung up his chef's hat and carving knife in 1991 after 54 years of serving up a local legend. With the help of the Illinois Route 66 Preservation Committee, Ernie's Pig Hip restaurant was transformed into a Route 66/Pig Hip Museum in late spring 2003, with 700 attending opening day. The Pig Hip's slogan, "The sandwich with the secret sauce: It made its way by the way it's made," was a fitting tribute to Ernie Edwards and his famous sandwich.

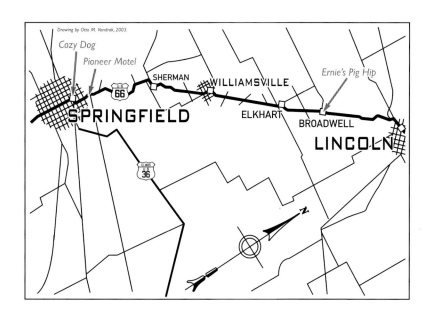

PIONEER MOTEL, SPRINGFIELD
c. 1940s

The classic Pioneer Motel sits on the north end of Springfield, beckoning to cars passing by on historic 66. This small motel was built in the 1940s close to Route 66 and the Route 66 city bypass and was highly rated by AAA. The Pioneer initially consisted of 12 units arranged in the classic L-shape style, with parking in front of each room. Sometime after the original construction, an archway was built over the driveway at the front office for guest safety, and a living room was added to the office space. At one time a small motel existed adjacent to the Pioneer but was eventually purchased by the owners of the Pioneer. The added rooms increased the Pioneer's total guest rooms to 21. The motel currently rents many units out by the month but keeps a few open for overnight guests looking to spend the night at a vintage Route 66 motel. One of the current owners, Teresa Roberts, says plans are in the works to renovate the motel. This, she says, will "hopefully attract more interest to the Pioneer Motel from travelers and fans of Route 66." Although the motel has gone through several ownership changes over the years, the name was never changed and to this day the classic MOTEL sign tower above the office continues to greet guests.

COZY DOG DRIVE IN, SPRINGFIELD
c. 1950

Ed Waldmire Jr. and his friend Don Strand developed the Cozy Dog while stationed in Amarillo, Texas, during World War II. To earn extra money, Ed sold the new-fangled food—a delectable combination of a hot dog on a stick dipped in special batter and French-fried—at the USO club and at the base PX. The "Crusty Curs," as they were first known, quickly became a local favorite. After Ed's discharge from the military he introduced the "dogs" to the public at the 1946 Illinois State Fair; they were such a hit that Ed decided to sell his new fast food in his hometown of Springfield, Illinois.

The first Cozy Dog stand was opened at the Lake Springfield beach house on June 16 of that same year. At the insistence of his wife Virginia, who wondered who would eat something called a "Crusty Cur," Ed began kicking around ideas for a new name. After much painstaking thought, "Cozy Dog" was settled upon. A second Cozy Dog stand was opened on Ash and MacArthur in Springfield, and in 1950 Waldmire moved into a building that shared seating with the local Dairy Queen. In 1976, Ed's son Buz and daughter-in-law Sue leased the restaurant from Ed. After their divorce, Buz sold his half to Sue, who has run the restaurant ever since. The Cozy Dog moved to its current location at 2935 South 6th Street in 1996 and sits partially on the property of the former Route 66 landmark Lincoln Motel.

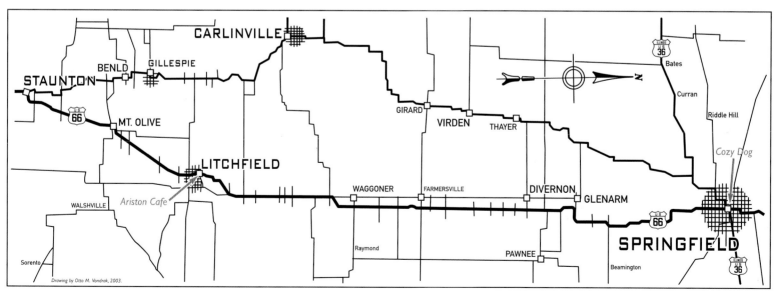

Drawing by Otto M. Vondrak, 2003.

ARISTON CAFÉ, LITCHFIELD
c. 1935

Ariston Café, opened by Pete Adam in the town of Carlinville in 1924, consisted of a small café with a few gas pumps out front. In 1926, Route 66 was given official designation and routed through the small Illinois town, and Adam's business flourished. In 1931, however, Highway 66 was re-routed east through Litchfield and business suffered. Not one to give up, Pete moved the Ariston to Litchfield. Business boomed again and in 1935 he found it necessary to construct a larger building. This "new" café, which holds more than 100 hungry customers, stands today pretty much as it did when it was built almost 70 years ago. Over the years, 66 was rerouted several times through Litchfield. Each change made it necessary to move the front door of the restaurant to keep it facing the road. As fate would have it, with the last realignment the restaurant entrance wound up at the original front location.

The Ariston is a well-known stop along Route 66 and has been a family-run operation since opening its doors. Nick and Demi Adam are proud of the café's history and its connection with the Mother Road, and continue the fine tradition that began 80 years ago. "We continue to believe in offering the highest quality selection of food, while providing the first-rate service that you expect," they say, "and at a price that continues to bring our valued customers back time and time again."

MISSOURI

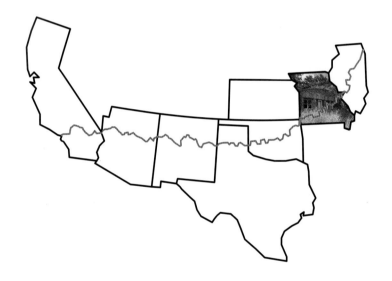

Route 66 leaves the Illinois plains and crosses into Missouri at the Mississippi River. It then cuts diagonally across Missouri from St. Louis to the high plains southwest of Springfield. As it slices through the Ozarks, the highway follows approximately the same route as a stage line established by the U.S. government two decades before the Civil War. During the Civil War, this trail was an important military thoroughfare traveled by Union and Confederate troops alike. It was during that time the federal government installed a telegraph line along the road with stations at St. Louis, Rolla, Lebanon, Marshfield, and Springfield. The old stage line, previously known as the Kickapoo Trail, the Osage Trace, the Springfield Road, and the Military Road, thus became known as the Old Wire Road or Telegraph Road.

At Springfield, the road connected with what would become the Ozark Trail, headed west, and eventually terminated in Santa Rosa, New Mexico. The Ozark Trails Association established the Ozark Trail in 1915, and in August 1922, the newly formed Missouri State Highway Commission designated seven roads totaling about 1,500 miles as primary roads throughout the state, including State Route 14, the future U.S. Highway 66, laid on the former Old Wire Road. Work on the new highway progressed at a rapid pace, and on January 5, 1931, the last section of hard top was completed in Pulaski County, making Missouri the third of the eight Route 66 states to complete its paving through the entire state.

The new road helped Missouri flourish and become one of the most popular vacation destinations in the country. Rivers, lakes, and a wealth of forestland attracted sportsmen from around the nation. Travelers and vacationers alike found an abundance of motels, resorts, and lodges to choose from. These vacation destinations came in all sizes and shapes, but none were more recognizable than the stylized stone or "rocked" buildings that proliferated in the Ozarks.

Highly skilled "rock men," as they were called, carefully cut and placed slabs of colorful sandstone over the frames of buildings, creating the unique look often called "giraffe stone." At the height of its popularity in the late 1930s and into the late 1940s, scores of motels, cafés, gas stations, and homes were rocked in this style. Many examples of this style still exist along Route 66 in the Ozarks region, including the Wagon Wheel Motel featured in this chapter.

Also popular in Missouri were the abundant caves and caverns that became tourist attractions over the years. Signs painted on barns to advertise the caverns became common sights throughout the Midwest on Route 66. By the time travelers arrived in Missouri, they were almost literally brainwashed into stopping. As an incentive, one cave owner, Lester Dills of Meremec Caverns in Stanton, offered to paint farmers' barns for free if they allowed him to advertise on them. Not many refused his offer.

As in the other states through which Route 66 passes, the road underwent many alignment changes in Missouri. Roads were straightened to make them safer, towns were bypassed to create faster routes, and two-lane Route 66 was eventually upgraded to four lanes. With the passage of the Federal Highway Aid Act in 1956, Missouri began work almost immediately on its new Interstate. Lebanon holds the dubious honor of being the first town in Missouri to be bypassed by the new highway. By the dawn of the 1980s Interstate 44 had replaced most of Route 66 across the Show-Me State; a section of the highway at Devils Elbow was the last to be bypassed in 1981. Even so, many surviving stretches of old Route 66 still exist today and can be driven and explored. Many of the small towns and villages there still retain that old-time feel and vintage charm of the Mother Road's glory days. They're all just an Interstate exit away.

THE DIAMONDS, VILLA RIDGE
c. 1948

Location, location, location—the key to success for any restaurant. At the junction of Routes 50, 66, and 100, The Diamonds utilized all three. Spencer Groff knew he had an envious location when he opened the first Diamonds on July 3, 1927. As word spread the restaurant quickly became known from coast to coast for fine food and courteous service. In 1948 a spectacular fire destroyed the original Diamonds and traffic was brought to a halt in both directions on Route 66 for hours as smoke covered the road. Groff and business partner Louis Eckelkamp (who also owned the nearby Gardenway Motel) rebuilt the Diamonds in an ultramodern streamlined style alongside 25 cottages and a swimming pool. In 1967 Interstate 44 bypassed the area and The Diamonds and its facilities were moved to new buildings farther east near the I-44 access ramp at Gray Summit. Interstate construction also forced the closure of the Tri-County Truck Stop 20 miles west in Sullivan. Owners Arla and Roscoe Reed in 1971 chose the abandoned Diamonds building to house the new Tri-County Truck Stop. Ironically, the relocated Diamonds Restaurant, once billed as the "World's Largest Roadside Restaurant," is now closed and abandoned, while the Tri-County Truck Stop remains open on the site of the second Diamonds, and continues to serve hungry truckers and tourists traveling I-44 and Route 66.

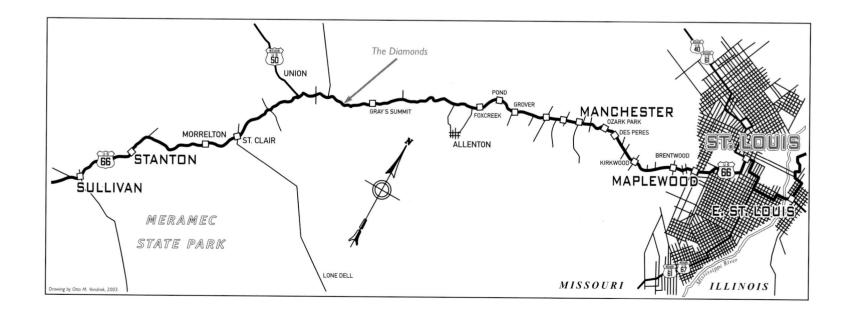

Drawing by Otto M. Vondrak, 2003.

WAGON WHEEL MOTEL, CUBA
c. 1934

The Wagon Wheel Motel on the eastern end of Cuba is one of the most recognizable landmarks on Route 66. Originally known as the Wagon Wheel Cabin Court, it was built by Robert and Margaret Martin, with local stonemason Leo Friescenhan hired as designer and construction supervisor. Originally a nine-room motel, Ozark Stone and brick trim on the windows and porches give it the classic "rocked" look that was popular in the region. The Wagon Wheel once boasted "All modern steam heated, fireproof cottages," as was printed on the back of this postcard. In the 1930s rooms rented for $1.50 and up per night. By 1946 the motel had expanded to 14 units, a number that grew to 18 when the garages were enclosed and converted. A service station and 24-hour café were also on the property, but were owned independently of the motel.

When I-44 bypassed the area in the late 1960s the motel's future looked bleak, but the Wagon Wheel managed to hang on. The motel has had several owners during its lifetime (one of them, a Mr. Mathis, designed the very recognizable neon sign), but Harold and Pauline Armstrong, owners for more than 40 years, attribute continued success to clean, quiet rooms at a great price. Venerable longtime caretaker Roy Mudd, who has been tending to the property for forty years, is as much a part of the classic motel as the neon sign and the Ozark stone.

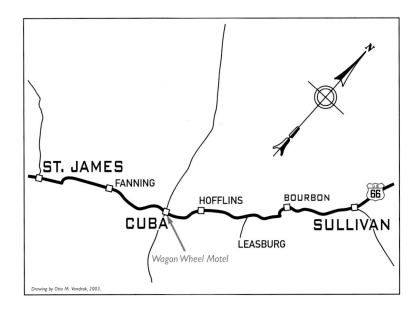

Drawing by Otto M. Vondrak, 2003.

ROLLA
c. 1940s

Rolla originated in 1855 when a group of contractors engaged in construction of the St. Louis, San Francisco Railway (aka "the Frisco") selected the area for supply warehouses and a railway office. According to legend, a local resident named George Coopedge, who was homesick for his native North Carolina, suggested the name Raleigh. The name was accepted and the decision was made to spell it exactly the way George pronounced it. The concrete paving of two-lane Route 66 through Missouri was completed in 1931 and was greeted by the citizens of Rolla with a huge public celebration that included a grand parade. There was cause for a celebration as the new and improved roadway meant increased traffic through town, which resulted in a much-needed boost for business at the local cafés, service stations, and motels that lined the town's main street. A couple of miles west of town in 1925, on the site of an old pioneer cabin, was built the Old Homestead, which today stands as one of the country's first truck stops.

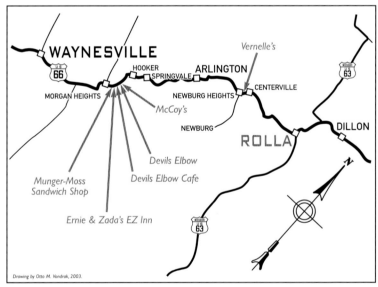

VERNELLE'S MOTEL, NEWBURG
c. 1952

In 1938 E. P. Gasser built a store, filling station, novelty shop, and six cabins on this property and named it Gasser Tourist Court. Fred and Vernelle Gasser bought the property from Fred's uncle in 1952 and added a restaurant and motel there. The restaurant seated 100 people and was well known for chicken-fried steak and open-faced roast beef sandwiches. The expansion of Route 66 to four lanes in 1957 necessitated the relocation of the restaurant and several other buildings. The motel was bought by Nye Goodridge in the early 1960s and is still owned and operated by his son Ed, who once worked in the restaurant as a cook and did "a little bit of everything" while his wife Jean worked as a waitress. According to

Ed, the restaurant was torn down around 1968 when Interstate 44 came through. Three units were added to the motel, however, bringing the total to 17.

Once again, Vernelle's, which has endured its share of setbacks, is on shaky ground. The state of Missouri deemed unsafe I-44 in this area, and announced that it will relocate it behind the motel, a project scheduled to take several years. Sadly, this will leave Vernelle's and its sign with no visibility from the Interstate and most likely will mark the end of another classic family-operated Route 66 motel. "We're going to be off the road," says Ed. "No visibility here at all. They are cutting our throats." Progress is a matter of opinion. Just ask Ed.

DEVILS ELBOW
c. 1939

Devils Elbow is a quiet, picturesque village on the Big Piney River about 20 miles west of Rolla. Listed as one of Missouri's top scenic spots, this Ozarks town was named by lumberjacks who floated logs down to this treacherous portion of the river. The logs would often jam at the bend and cause long delays, leading the rafters to comment that the river at this point had a "devil of an elbow."

A block east of the bridge leading into Devils Elbow sits the Elbow Inn (originally Munger-Moss Sandwich Shop). Across the bridge is the site of the old Devils Elbow Café and the Conoco station built by Dwight Rench in 1932. The café and station were at one time affiliated with the nearby Cedar Lodge, 10 cabins boasting private cooking facilities. The café housed the local post office from 1931 to 1941, and in later years was transformed into a tavern called The Hideaway, which burned to the ground in the late 1950s. A block from the café was McCoy's Store and Camp, an old-fashioned general store built by Charles McCoy in 1941. In addition to selling fishing tackle and sporting goods, McCoy's rented boats for use on the Big Piney, as well as six small sleeping rooms upstairs; the

Devils Elbow Cafe
Devils Elbow, Mo.

Devils Elbow Cafe
Devils Elbow, Mo

owners lived in a four-bedroom apartment downstairs behind the store. In 1948 seven small cabins were added, but McCoy's closed in 1954 and was turned into an apartment building.

That year, McCoy's son-in-law, Atholl "Jiggs" Miller, and his wife Dorothy built Millers Market, and sold camping essentials, dry goods, and gasoline. Jiggs was the postmaster until 1982 when he sold the market to Terry and Marilyn Allman, who operated the store as Allman's Market until October 2001, when the property was sold to Phil Sheldon, who changed the name to Sheldon's Market. Sheldon had managed The Hideaway for a year before entering the army in

1942. About a mile west of downtown sat Ernie and Zada's Inn, also known as the E-Z Inn. Built in the late 1930s it consisted of a Sinclair station, restaurant, and cabins and had a wild reputation as a honky-tonk. It closed after only a few years of operation, according to Sheldon. The building that once served as the gas station and restaurant is now a private residence.

In 1943 Route 66 bypassed the town was to accommodate heavy military traffic from nearby Fort Leonard Wood, and in the early 1980s Interstate 44 completely left Devils Elbow behind.

DANCING, FISHING, HUNTING, SHADY TRAILER CAMP, DINNERS, LUNCHES, BEER MODERN CABINS WITH IN-SPR. MATTRESS

E161   ERNIE & ZADA'S INN   HI-WAY 66   1 MILE WEST OF   DEVIL'S ELBOW, MO.   Schuster Studio Hermann, Mo.

McCOY'S AT DEVIL'S ELBOW, MO.

MUNGER-MOSS
SANDWICH SHOP, DEVILS ELBOW
c. 1936

Nelle Munger and Emmett Moss built the Munger-Moss Sandwich Shop in 1936 soon after they married. The café was built on a piece of land that sits next to the picturesque bridge at the Big Piney River. Route 66 bypassed this location in 1943 when a new four-lane section was completed to accommodate heavy military traffic from nearby Fort Leonard Wood. As a result of the realignment, tourist traffic through the area was drastically reduced and business slowed to a crawl. The Munger-Moss Sandwich Shop then moved, along with its original owners, to a new location west of Devils Elbow in the town of Lebanon. In 1946, Paul and Nadine Thompson bought and reopened the old location and changed the name of the café to the Elbow Inn, which they successfully operated well into the 1960s. After its closure the café sat empty and at one time served as a private residence. It was reopened in 1997, again as the Elbow Inn, and has since gained quite a reputation for its outstanding barbecue.

S663   BIG PINEY RIVER,   HI-WAY 66,   DEVIL'S ELBOW   Schuster Studio

WAYNESVILLE
c. 1940s

Waynesville was established in 1833 as a simple trading post for settlers and trappers on the Roubidoux River, and was named for General "Mad" Anthony Wayne, a hero of the Revolutionary War. The stretch of Route 66 in this area can be traced back to the early 1800s when an overland trail was established between St. Louis and Springfield. The trail's various names spell out its history: Kickapoo Trail, the Osage Trace, Old Wire Road, Old Springfield Road, Highway 14, and eventually U.S Highway 66.

Many buildings in Waynesville survive from the 1920s and 1930s, including the former Bell Hotel (now Waynesville Memorial Chapel) built by Robert Bell. In anticipation of the coming tourist trade from the new Highway 66, Bell expanded his home in 1925 and turned it into the Bell Hotel. It operated until 1937 under the slogan "Every Facility for the Traveler's Pleasure – Old Southern Hospitality." Through the hard times of the 1920s and 1930s Waynesville's status as the seat of Pulaski County, combined with the ever-increasing tourist travel on Route 66, kept the town alive. In 1941 the construction of nearby Fort Leonard Wood brought thousands of military and construction workers to the area, and as World War II unfolded Waynesville became the primary place of recreation for men and women stationed on the base. Since then, Waynesville has had its share of ups and downs, good times and bad, but the friendliness and small-town ways have remained constant.

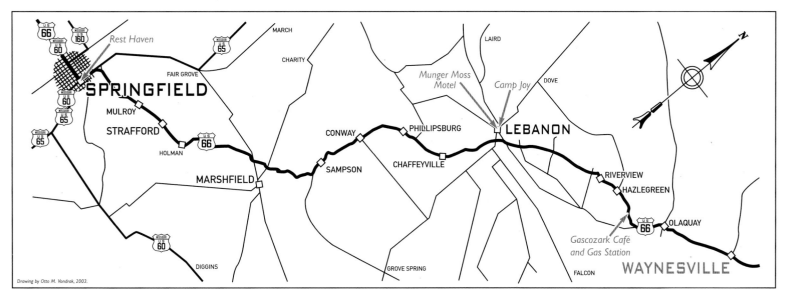

Drawing by Otto M. Vondrak, 2003.

GASCOZARK CAFÉ
AND GAS STATION, GASCOZARK
c. 1939

In 1931, Frank A. Jones built the Gascozark Café and Gas Station, which he owned and operated along with a popular tourist and fishing resort on the nearby Gasconade River. Jones, who originally settled in the area in the 1920s, in fact coined the town name "Gascozark" as a combination of *Gasconade* and Ozark. The former refers to the Gascony region of France that lent its name to the nearby river; the latter is a distortion of the French *Aux Arc. Aux* (sounds like "oh") means "to" and *arc* is short for one of the region's native tribes. "Ozark," hence, literally means "to the Arkansas."

As tourist traffic on Route 66 steadily increased, so did business at the café and Jones soon made additions to the main building. In the mid-1930s Rudy and Clara Schuermann bought and took over the business. In 1939 the Schuermanns hired a Mr. Lillard, a "rock man," who added the large Ozark stones around the front and sides to alleviate the patchy look of the main building and its add-ons. In the 1940s the Gascozark Café and Gas Station became a regular stop on the Greyhound bus line, providing a substantial boost in business. In the 1950s another transformation to the café took place when it became a local hot spot known as the Spinning Wheel Tavern. In later years the building served as a private residence but as of this writing it sits vacant.

CAMP JOY, LEBANON
c. 1930

Leaving Nebraska City, Nebraska, behind, Ernis and Lois Spears, accompanied by Ernis' parents, traveled back and forth on the new U. S. Highway 66 during the late 1920s in search of the perfect spot for a new tourist camp. Upon arriving in each town the two couples surveyed the area for possibilities, often spending days in one spot, counting passing cars. They found what they were looking for in Lebanon. Camp Joy, which began with 50-cents-a-night tent rentals, was so successful that Ernis and his father Charles built cabins. Eventually, attached carports were converted to drive-in garages and then to more rooms. As tourist travel increased so did tourist demands, and indoor plumbing in each cabin replaced a communal bathhouse.

By the end of 1935 Camp Joy featured 24 cabins that rented for $1.25 to $4, depending on the number of rooms. A gas station and café were added but were eventually moved to accommodate even more cabins. A drive-through archway read, "Camp Joy" on the entrance side and "Teach your baby to say Camp Joy" on the exit side. According to Joy Spears Fishel, Ernis and Lois's daughter, customers in the early days seemed more like friends than customers: "In the evenings after supper, people would get out and visit. TV made a big difference. TV and air conditioning. After those came in people didn't want to get together anymore." The Spears owned and operated the property until 1971. The few cabins still standing are now rented on a monthly basis

MUNGER MOSS MOTEL, LEBANON
c. 1950s

Jesse and Pete Hudson, onetime owners of the Munger Moss Sandwich Shop in Devils Elbow, relocated in Lebanon after Devils Elbow was bypassed. Property in Lebanon was purchased in 1945 and the Munger Moss Motor Court was built in 1946 and originally consisted of seven buildings housing two units each and a garage. Rooms rented for $3 a night. Eleven more buildings were eventually added along the semicircular driveway, adding 44 new rooms. As tourist business increased during the postwar era so did demand for more rooms. As with many motels of the era, the attached garages were converted into rooms. Television came to the area in the early 1950s and tacked an extra 50 cents to the room rate. A swimming pool, new office, and sign were added in the late 1950s; all three are still in use today.

Bob and Ramona Lehman bought the motel in 1971 and have been its caretakers ever since. Ramona has gloriously decorated a few of the rooms with Route 66 themes: Room 18 is the famous Coral Court Room, a must see for Route 66 enthusiasts. Room 66 is, of course, the Munger Moss Historic Room, filled with old photos and memorabilia. Illinois, Kansas, Oklahoma, and Missouri all have rooms decorated in their honor, and the motel is one of the cleanest and well kept along all of Route 66.

REST HAVEN
MOTOR COURT
SPRINGFIELD, MO.

MAY PHOTO

REST HAVEN MOTOR COURT, SPRINGFIELD
c. 1947

The Rest Haven Motor Court was built in 1947 by Hillary and Mary Brightwell and originally consisted of four rock cottages containing two rooms each, and a Phillips 66 service station out front. In 1953 a new two-story sign was added and is said to use 900 individual light bulbs. Many of the motels on Route 66 expanded at a furious pace during the postwar period and the Rest Haven was no exception. Ten more rock cottages were added in 1952, and in 1955 an additional 10 were built to meet the ever-growing demand. By that time the Rest Haven offered "100% Refrigerated Air Conditioning," telephones, free radios, ice, a well-equipped playground, and was

recommended by Duncan Hines. The service station out front was dismantled in 1955 and reassembled at the rear of the property; today it is used for storage. In the early 1960s the gaps between the original four cottages were filled in to add three more rooms. A swimming pool was also installed in the 1960s. Hillary and Mary owned the motel and lived on site until 1979 when, after 32 years of greeting guests, they retired. In 1980 the Rest Haven was purchased by Mr. and Mrs. Pendya, who have been caretakers ever since. The Rest Haven remains a fine example of the well-kept, mom-and-pop motels that have survived despite the road's demise.

LOG CITY CAMP, AVILLA
c. 1940s

In 1926 Carl Stansbury built several log cabins 14 1/2 miles east of Carthage, Missouri, to start a business utilizing trees he cut down while clearing the land. Out front of Log City Camp he built a café made of stone, a gas station, and a store. By 1935 Stansbury had built "fourteen modern cottages with conveniences" that rented for $1 to $3 a night. The camp eventually expanded to include 16 cottages and cabins. On the back of this postcard Log City Camp advertised a "Dining room with coffee shop, air conditioned by washed air, serving excellent food at popular prices. You Name It, We've Got It." Log City also boasted Beautyrest mattresses in each cabin.

Two years after building Log City, rivals built the Forest Park Camp across the highway. Forest Park at the time comprised 10 rock cabins. Not to be outdone, Stansbury added three rock cabins of his own. When the owners of Forest Park built a café, Stansbury added a coffee shop to the Log City Camp. Stansbury also added a dining room, prompting his rivals across the highway to establish a tavern and dance hall. This "friendly" competition went on for years, with the owners of each camp trying to outdo the other. Eventually the new Interstate bypassed both camps. Just a single rock cabin remains across the highway at the former Forest Park Camp.

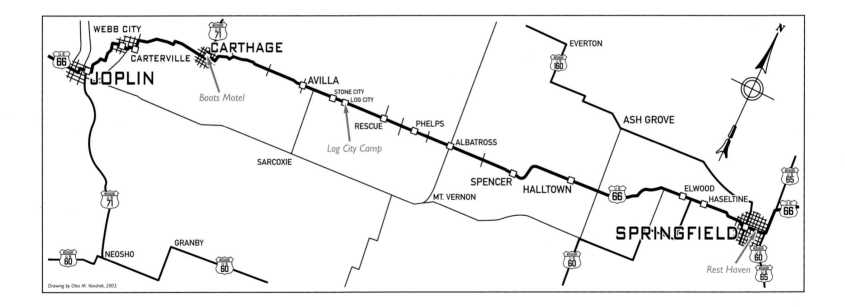

Drawing by Otto M. Vondrak, 2003.

LOG CITY CAMP
14½ MILES EAST OF CARTHAGE M.
ON HIGHWAY 66

DINING ROOM
LOG CITY CAMP
BLAKE
Photo

COTTAGE AT LOG CITY CAMP
ON HIGHWAY 66
14½ MILES EAST OF
CARTHAGE MO.

BOOTS COURT, CARTHAGE
c. 1949

Situated at the corner of Route 66 and Highway 71 at the so-called "Crossroads of America" sits the Boots Motel, one of the most recognizable landmarks on all of Route 66. Built by Arthur Boots in 1939, the distinctly streamline moderne motel began with four units of two rooms each. Classic pink and green neon follow the graceful lines of the motel, and a covered driveway allows guests to park next to their rooms. A Mobil station that once sat out front was eliminated to make space for more rooms. Early advertising boasted of "A radio in every room," and Clark Gable is rumored to have stayed in Room 6 and signed the guest book, "Clark Gable and Party."

In 1942 Ples Nelly bought the Boots Motel and added five rooms at the rear of the complex. In 1948, Ruben and Rachel Asplin bought the property, longing to leave the cold winters of Minnesota behind. After Ruben's death, Rachel continued to run the motel until her death in 1991 at the age of 91. Current owner John Ferguson rents rooms on a weekly basis only, but still turns on the classic neon every night. The motel's listing on the National Register of Historic Places would be a shoo-in if not for the nonoriginal pitched roof that was added in later years. At the time of this writing Ferguson was hoping for a buyer to restore the Boots to its former glory.

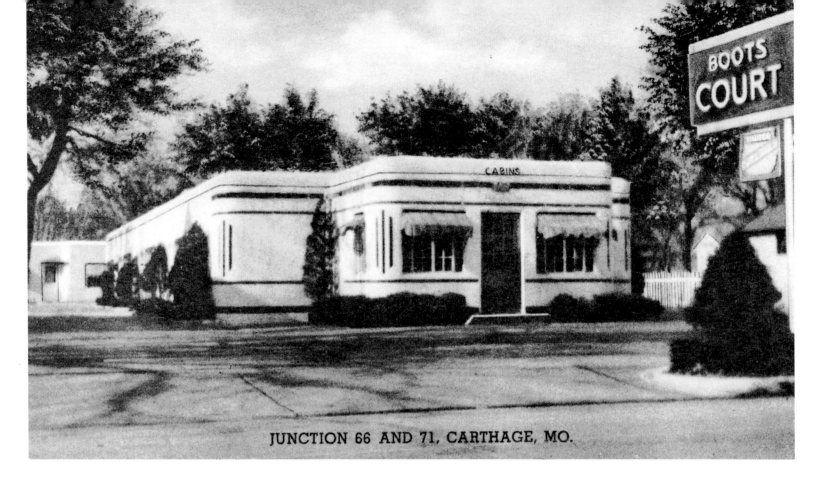

JUNCTION 66 AND 71, CARTHAGE, MO.

KANSAS

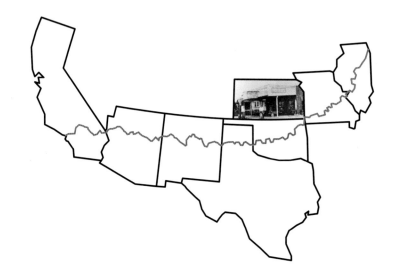

Of the 2,400 miles of Route 66 from Chicago to Los Angeles, Kansas accounts for a mere 13.2 miles. While cattle and the railroad played major roles in the economics of the region, this area of the state was ore-mining country from 1876 to around 1960. One lucky miner is said to have uncovered his fortune while sliding into first base during a baseball game. He quickly covered it up, leased the land that night, and began digging the next morning.

The first town one encounters along Route 66 in Kansas is Galena. Just before entering Galena is an area that looks a bit like a war-torn battle zone. Known as "Hell's Half Acre," piles of mining debris known as "chat" fill the landscape, a sobering reminder of past mining operations and the devastation it caused to the local environment. Many bloody union battles were also staged and fought in the region.

Just a few miles down 66 is Riverton, the onetime home of the world-famous Spring River Inn. Built in 1905, the Spring River began operation as a restaurant in 1952 and was destroyed by fire in the late 1990s. Still farther down the highway is Baxter Springs, "The First Cow Town in Kansas" and the site of the Baxter Springs Massacre. In October 1863 Lieutenant William Quantrill's Confederate troops, dressed in Union Army uniforms, ambushed an unknowing Union detachment and wagon train approaching the fort. One hundred three Union soldiers were killed, along with three Confederate soldiers. All are buried in a mass grave near the former site of the fort.

This part of Kansas boasts an abundance of rich and colorful history in which U.S Highway 66 played a major part. Tales of outlaw legends abound in these parts, including a well-known Jesse James bank robbery in the 1870s and frequent appearances by Bonnie Parker and Clyde Barrow more than 60 years later.

As the mining industry slowly dwindled the economy was bolstered by the influx of westbound travelers on Route 66. All three Kansas towns located along the Mother Road served travelers well. Those 13.2 miles in Kansas provide a virtual microcosm of the entire eight-state route; Galena, Riverton, and Baxter Springs were prime examples of the hundreds of small towns that dotted the length of the highway. During the Mother Road's heyday, their main streets were full of tourists filling their automobiles with gas or catching a quick bite at local cafés. Today, the streets are lined with classic architecture. Many a weary traveler too tired to drive another couple of miles to Oklahoma spent the night at Jayhawk Court in Riverton or the Capistrano Motel or Baxter Modern Cabins in Baxter Springs.

The lucrative tourist trade came to a sudden end when Interstate construction was completed in the area in the early 1960s, connecting I-44 in Missouri to the Will Rogers Turnpike in Oklahoma and leaving Kansas high and dry. In fact, Kansas holds the dubious distinction of being the only Route 66 state to be completely bypassed by the Interstate. It is also the only state not represented in Bobby Troup's hit song "Get Your Kicks on Route 66." The old route through Kansas remained a state road, however, and is today designated Kansas 66. Local residents are proud of their 13.2 miles and work hard to keep and preserve what is left.

GALENA
c. 1950s

Route 66 enters Galena over a gracefully curved overpass down to Front Street. After about half a mile, it takes a sharp left-hand turn onto Main Street. At one time Galena, named for a type of lead ore that often contained silver, had a reputation as a rowdy, untamed mining town complete with gamblers, swindlers, and drunkards. Main Street during the early 1900s mining boom was known as "Red Hot Street" and was full of saloons, gambling joints, and bawdy houses, all open 24 hours. Traveling down the sleepy Main Street today one would be hard-pressed to see any evidence of Galena's wild past. In 1935 striking United Mine Workers blocked Route 66 in front of the Eagle Picher Smelter and shot at drivers who ignored their commands. Sheriffs rerouted traffic and the governor declared martial law and sent in the National Guard. Labor unrest continued and reached a climax in 1937 when nine men were shot while demonstrating against union organization efforts. During the 1940s and 1950s local roadside businesses enjoyed steady streams of traffic and customers as America's Main Street also happened to be Galena's Main Street. Today, Main Street is home to a few local businesses but the damage caused by a dwindling mining industry and a Route 66 bypass is evident in the abandoned brick buildings that line the street. During the mining boom Galena's population ran as high as 25,000; today it hovers at around 4,000.

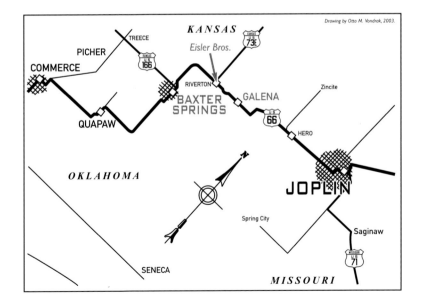

EISLER BROTHERS MARKET, RIVERTON
c. 1930s

On March 20, 1925 Leo Williams and his wife Lora opened a small roadside store on what was to become U.S. Highway 66 through Riverton. Fashioned after the "general" stores of the era, the Williams' store carried everything from clothes and shoes to milk, eggs, and fresh meat, as well as chili and barbecued beef that were cooked in a pit out back. A regulation croquet court was built on a lot adjacent to the store complete with lights for night play. Local tournaments became popular among area residents. As traffic continued to grow, business flourished and the court was dismantled to accommodate a parking lot.

In 1945 Leo leased the store to Lloyd Paxton and purchased a roller rink in nearby Galena. When Paxton's lease expired, Lora, then a widow, returned to manage the store as Lora Williams' AG Food Market. In 1971 Lora transferred ownership of the property to her daughter, Jane. Joe and Isabelle Eisler bought the business from Thelma Ball in 1973 and continue to operate it as a store and deli with nephew Scott Nelson (president of the Kansas Route 66 Association) as manager. Although Interstate 44 bypassed this area in 1961 the store continues to survive as a result of its strong local customer base and the current crop of Route 66 explorers.

BAXTER SPRINGS
c. 1940s

Baxter Springs was founded when John Baxter and his family settled there in 1849. The nearby mineral springs are said to have miraculous healing powers and were known to the Osage Indians who long made regular trips there. As white settlers arrived in the area word of the springs spread and their popularity exploded. To accommodate the visitors, John Baxter opened an inn and tavern called Baxter's Place, but he was brutally murdered in a land dispute in 1859.

Baxter Springs became known as the "First Cow Town in Kansas" when in 1867 the first herd of longhorns from Texas were driven there and sold to buyers who took the cattle to markets farther north. Baxter Springs gained a rough-and-tumble reputation and the moniker "The toughest town on earth." From 1867 to 1872, as the cattle trade prospered, gunfights and public hangings became commonplace. When rail lines were built into Texas, cattle no longer had to be driven north, and law and order were finally restored. Mining became the region's chief industry with the discovery of lead and zinc in nearby Picher, Oklahoma. As mining faded, so did the local economy. Through the years Baxter Springs has managed to survive and with the increased auto travel on Route 66 in the postwar period the town made a strong comeback. At one point Baxter Springs, because of its central location, was served by five large trucking companies and was used as an eight-state distribution point and maintenance depot for a major freight company.

U.S. 66 AND MAIN STREET — BAXTER SPRINGS, KANSAS D-1

OKLAHOMA

Route 66 was born in Oklahoma and its father was Cyrus Avery, a Tulsa businessman who became the state's first highway commissioner in 1913. After several years of lobbying for a national highway system, his hard work and perseverance paid off. In 1925 a letter from U.S. Secretary of Agriculture Howard Gore announcing the creation of a special board to "design and number a system of routes of interstate and national importance" arrived at his door. Gore asked Avery to act as a consultant to the American Association of State Highway Officials, which Avery persuaded to route the new highway through Oklahoma, Texas, New Mexico, Arizona, and into California. Prior to Avery's lobbying the new highway's path was to travel through Kansas and Colorado on its way to California. After much debate, Avery also convinced the board to settle on the number 66 for the new Chicago-to-Los Angeles highway.

In the early 1930s drought, dust storms, and the Great Depression triggered a mass migration of Texas, Arkansas, Kansas, and Colorado farmers to head for California's promised land. More than 200,000 of these Dust Bowl migrants fled through Oklahoma on Highway 66. John Steinbeck, in his Pulitzer Prize–winning novel, *The Grapes of Wrath,* forever immortalized to the world the plight of the Oklahoma farmer or "Okie." One can hardly forget the visual impact characterized in John Ford's motion picture adaptation of three generations of the Joad family, tightly packed into their cut-down Hudson Super Six sedan, and struggling to cross the dry plains, desert, and mountains to reach California. "66 is the path of a people in flight, refugees from dust and shrinking land, from the thunder of tractors and shrinking ownership," wrote Steinbeck, "they come into 66 from the tributary side roads, from the wagon tracks and the rutted country roads. 66 is the mother road, the road of flight."

The Turner Turnpike (Interstate 44) between Tulsa and Oklahoma City, bypassed 100 miles of the Mother Road and was the first major bypass on the route. In 1957 the Will Rogers Turnpike opened between Tulsa and Miami, leaving another 100 miles of Route 66 to fend for itself. In 1975 the four-lane section of Route 66 from Sayre to Erick was the last section in Oklahoma to lose its U.S. 66 designation to I-40.

The pathway of Route 66 in Oklahoma covers approximately 400 miles and travels somewhat diagonally across the heart of the state, slicing through mining, agricultural, industrial, and oil regions. Although 66 went through countless changes over the years in Oklahoma, there are still more drivable "original" portions of Route 66 in that state than any other.

MIAMI
c. 1930s

Miami, Oklahoma, was established in 1891. That much is certain. How it got its name is a different matter. Some say Wayland C. Lykins, a cattle rancher attracted to the region's plentiful grazing land got the townsite approved, and on March 2, 1891, Miami became the first chartered town in "Indian Territory," named by Lykins for the local tribe. Others say Miami started out as a trading post called "Jimtown" because it was near the homes of four local farmers named Jim. In 1890 to expedite mail delivery, arrangements were made with one of the farmers, Jim Palmer, to establish a post office. The name Miami was chosen in honor of Palmer's wife, who was of Miami Indian blood. No matter which story you believe, remember: Miami is pronounced *my-am-uh* not *my-am-ee.*

In 1922, a unique stretch of roadway was built between Miami and Afton. When it came time to pave the 10 miles between the two cities, the highway commissioners from Craig and Ottawa counties found they had half the money necessary. Since the Federal Highway Commission required the road to be paved for the county to receive federal funds but did not specify width, engineer George Klein suggested they make the road a single lane 9 feet wide paved all the way. In 1937, this stretch was finally bypassed and became the last section of Route 66 in Oklahoma to be completely paved. Portions of this so-called "Ribbon Highway" or "Sidewalk Highway" can still be driven today.

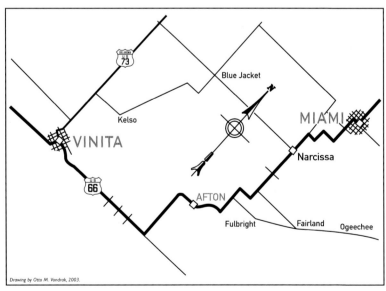

Drawing by Otto M. Vondrak, 2003.

AFTON
c. 1958

The small farming community of Afton was established in 1886 and given its name by railroad surveyor Anton Aires, who named the town after his daughter. Afton has many historic buildings lining its downtown area, including the old Palmer Hotel and the Rest Haven Motel. The Interstate bypass in 1957 and the decommissioning of Route 66 had a profoundly negative impact on Afton's economy. During the golden era of U.S. Highway 66, Afton was a thriving community with no less than six service stations and six motels lining its short stretch of Main Street. Today, there are very few survivors. On the outskirts of town stands the venerable Buffalo Ranch Trading Post, a landmark tourist stop built in 1953 by Russell and Aleene Kay with a budget of $5,000. The business eventually grew to include four buildings housing a trading post, western store, barbecue, dairy ranch, and a variety of livestock. The Buffalo Ranch closed its doors in 1997 when owner Aleene Albro (then remarried) died. The original buildings were torn down in 2002 and replaced with a new facility that includes a gas station and restaurant.

Afton is also home to Afton Station. From 1999 to the time of this writing, Laurel Kane has been restoring the 1930s-era gas station for use as a Route 66 visitors' center. Every attempt is being made to preserve the vintage flavor of the old service station, which originally sold Sunray DX petroleum products. An attached garage will serve as a museum for vintage automobiles.

MAIN STREET - HIGHWAY 66 - AFTON, OKLA.

VINITA
c. 1939

Vinita, Oklahoma is not only the oldest incorporated town in Oklahoma, it is the second oldest town in the state. Vinita was established in 1871 and, like so many other towns in this part of Oklahoma, was primarily known as a railroad community. Originally known as Downingville, the name was later changed to honor Vinnie Ream, the local sculptress commissioned to carve the statue of Abraham Lincoln now located in the U.S. Capitol Building in Washington, D.C. Colonel Elias C. Boudinot, a Cherokee and one of the town site's first promoters, was responsible for the name change. Boudinot's father and 34 others were responsible for selling the Cherokee ancestral lands in the Southeast to the federal government.

The Trail of Tears mass migration that resulted in 1838 brought thousands of relocated Cherokees to the area.

Several historic buildings survive in Vinita, including the fully restored shopping district. Vinita is also home to Clanton's Café, built in 1927 and now being run by the fourth generation of Clantons. Hotel Vinita and the Spraker Service Station also served Route 66 during its heyday and were added to the National Register of Historic Places in 1995. In addition, Will Rogers went to the Willie Halsell Institute in Vinita, and it's said that he felt more at home there than at any other school he attended.

CATOOSA INDIAN TRADING POST, CATOOSA
c. 1955

Chief Wolfe Robe Hunt and his wife, Glenal, opened their first trading post out of their home in Tulsa in 1936. Not long after, they moved the shop to 11th Street (Route 66) in Tulsa. They were so successful selling Osage beadwork and Indian curios that they soon expanded the business to include Navajo jewelry and Acoma pottery, and opened a second store in Catoosa. When the Turner Turnpike bypassed Route 66, the business suffered and Chief Wolfe Robe Hunt and his wife moved the business to the newer location in Catoosa the following year. Chief Wolfe Robe Hunt pooled resources with his brother-in-law, Hugh Davis (builder of the famous Blue Whale across

the street), and the two entered business together, adding a gas station and café and changing the name to the Catoosa Indian Trading Post. Davis sold his portion of the business back to Chief Wolfe Hunt Robe in 1957. After the death of Chief Wolfe Robe Hunt the old trading post lay empty for many years until 1990, when Dave Jennings and his wife Pam bought the property and reopened the business as Arrowood's Trading Post. The gas pumps and café were long gone and the lack of business forced the trading post to close its doors in the late 1990s. The original building currently houses an auto repair shop.

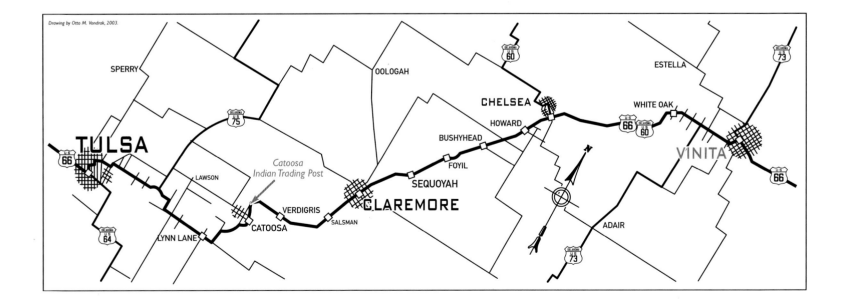

Drawing by Otto M. Vondrak, 2003.

SHADY REST COURT, WEST TULSA
c. 1942

The Shady Rest Court is located in West Tulsa in what was once a suburb called Red Fork. Red Fork was responsible for putting Tulsa on the map as the "Oil Capital of the World" when a large oil field was found there in 1901. Maurice Colpitts, a Tulsa plumbing inspector, built the front-gable-style Shady Rest Cabins in 1936. Each of the 13 units was built around a 10x12 frame just large enough for a bed and two people. Unlike those at many motels, the Shady Rest carports were never converted to rooms, adding to the historic value and vintage feel.

During the glory days of Route 66 the Shady Rest Court offered "The best of accommodations for your money. Innerspring mattresses and air cooled cabins." The Shady Rest has seen four owners and only recently fell into a state of disrepair. The units are now quite run down and rented on a monthly basis. There is some hope, though, for the venerable old motor court. The original sign is being renovated and improvements and repairs are slowly being made to each cabin, according to current manager, Lorie Murphy. She hopes the new owners will realize and understand the historic importance of the Shady Rest Court and restore it to its original appearance, when tired motorists gladly stopped here for a "shady rest."

SHADY REST COURT
TULSA, OKLAHOMA

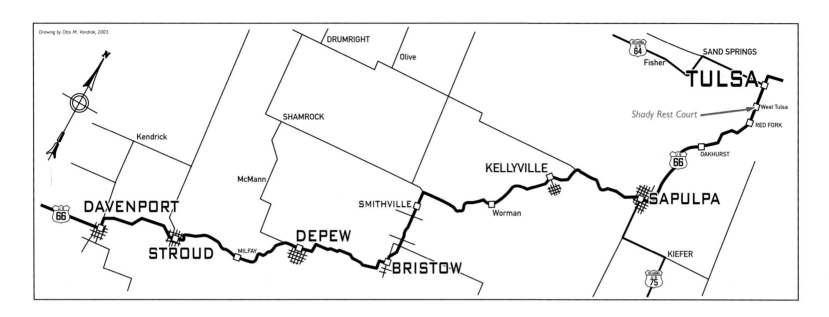

Drawing by Otto M. Vondrak, 2003.

VIEW FROM THE
CAPITOL BUILDING, OKLAHOMA CITY
c. 1935

Route 66 carried motorists directly in front of the Capitol Building in Oklahoma City, the only state capital on the entire route, via Lincoln Boulevard. Oklahoma City became the largest boomtown of the 1889 Land Rush when the region was opened for white settlement despite the promise of being "forever" set aside as "Indian Territory." On April 22 of that year, more than 10,000 people flocked to an area known as the Cherokee Strip between noon and sundown to stake claim to their land. Many of the settlers illegally camped out beforehand, hoping to get an advantage on the competition. These early birds were given the name "Sooners," a nickname still applied to University of Oklahoma sports teams and the state nickname "The Sooner State." A second boom took place during the depression years when oil was struck in the area. By 1946, more than 1,000 oil derricks were located in and around the city, many of which still produce oil to this day. Most of the vintage Route 66 charm in Oklahoma City is long gone, the cafés, diners, classic service stations, and motor courts but a fond memory. But if you spend time and look hard enough, there are still remnants of the Mother Road waiting to be discovered in Oklahoma City.

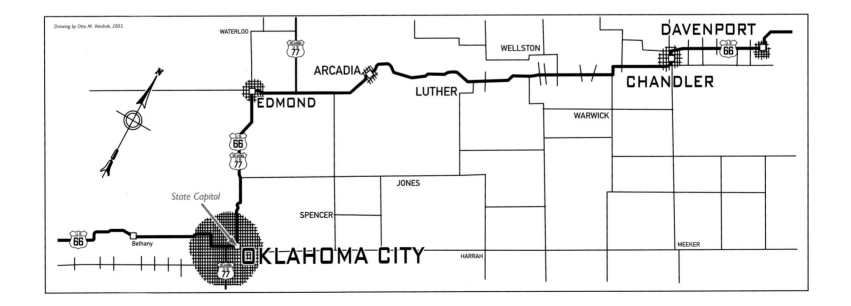

Drawing by Otto M. Vondrak, 2003.

HAMONS' COURT
(AKA LUCILLE'S), HYDRO
c. 1941

The original two-story building that eventually housed Hamons' Gas Station was built in 1927 by a man named Carl Ditmore of Hydro, Oklahoma. After a couple of years a five-unit motel was built behind the station. Carl and Lucille Hamons bought the Provine Station in 1941 and renamed it Hamons' Court. When construction of Interstate 40 in the area was completed in 1962, access to Hamons' Court was cut off and the couple closed the motel. Carl passed away in 1971. Lucille eventually changed the station's name to Lucille's, and in 1997 it was placed on the National Register of Historic Places (as the Provine Station). In 1999, Lucille was inducted in the Route 66 Hall of Fame at age of 84. The original Hamons' Court sign was shipped to the Smithsonian Institute in 2003.

Lucille passed away in August 2000; hundreds attended her funeral. Anyone would be hard-pressed to accurately describe Lucille, who was at once kind and generous, but also stubborn and forceful when fighting for something she believed in. Countless times she provided food to hungry travelers with no money or a free place to stay when their cars broke down. She fought heartily for an exit when the Interstate threatened to cut off her business. When the state told her they were trying to get rid of these small places along the highway, it only fueled her resolve. She lived on Route 66 for 59 years, serving and caring for thousands along the way. She truly earned the title "Mother of the Mother Road."

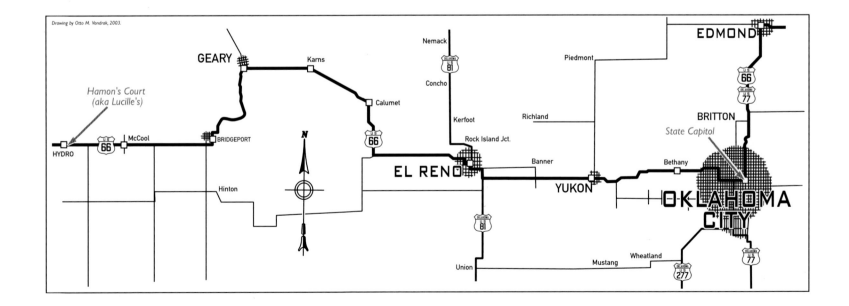

Drawing by Otto M. Vondrak, 2003.

COTTON BOLL MOTEL, CANUTE
c. 1960

The small community of Canute is home to one of the most photographed landmarks on all of Route 66. The Cotton Boll Motel is certainly not the oldest motel on the route, nor is it an architectural standout, but something about the classic red and white sign outlined in red and green neon attracts tourists from around the country. Woodrow and Viola Penick, both former cotton farmers, built the Cotton Boll in 1960, using the classic L-shape with parking in front of each unit. A central courtyard was replaced with a swimming pool in later years. The back of this postcard advertises, "16 units completely new and modern. Wall to wall carpets. Tile baths, free TV in rooms. Refrigerated Air-conditioning, baby cribs, laundry, complimentary coffee in rooms."

Business was "excellent," according to Viola, until 1970 when Interstate 40 bypassed Canute. Woodrow and Viola sold the motel in 1979. During the short oil boom in the early 1980s the Cotton Boll's new owners rented rooms to workers from nearby oil fields. In the mid-1990s the motel was purchased by Pat and Cheryl Webb, who turned the office and Room 1 into a private home. To area residents, the Cotton Boll's sign has become a symbol and a reminder of the days when America's Main Street rolled through town. While many of these locals feared the new owners would have the sign removed, the Webbs have no intention of bringing down the landmark. "This is a big part of their life," Pat says.

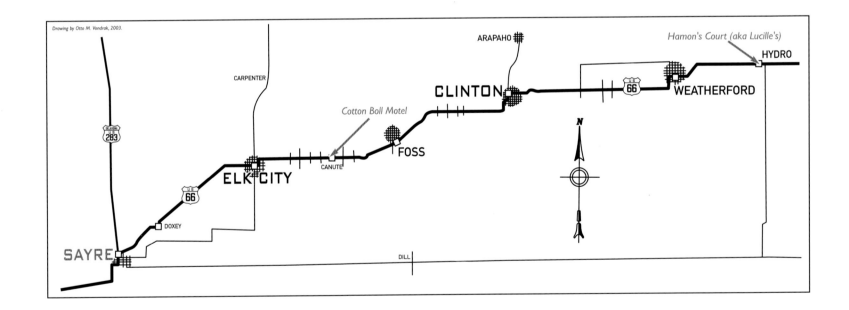

SAYRE
c. 1940

The Beckham County seat was named for Robert H. Sayre, a stockholder in the railroad that reached Sayre at its founding in 1901. The north fork of the Red River flows along the southern outskirts of the town, and at one time the area was developed into a public park that included several sandy beaches. The Beckham County Courthouse in this photograph appeared very briefly in John Ford's movie version of *The Grapes of Wrath*. Onetime heavyweight boxing champion of the world Jess Willard called Sayre home and ran a boarding house in town for many years.

In 1924, prior to the designation of U.S. Highway 66, a 2,600-foot-long timber bridge was constructed across the Red River to carry traffic on the newly designated State Highway 3. By 1926, the road carried the new 66 designation. With the increase of automobile traffic, the bridge needed fortification and in 1933 steel beams were incorporated. The revamped bridge remained in use until 1958 when a new bridge was opened on the new four-lane alignment. The remains of the original bridge, which burned in 1959, now sit on private property. Story has it that soon after the bridge burned and a barricade was constructed at the river bank, local high school kids would hang around the bridge site and frantically warn out-of-state drivers that "The Indians attacked and burned down the bridge. You'd better roll up your windows and head for the state line."

TEXAS

Route 66 crosses the pancake-like plains of the Texas panhandle, covering the 178 miles between Oklahoma and New Mexico. The panhandle is sometimes called the *Llano Estacado* or "Staked Plains," because early settlers in the area marked their routes by driving stakes into the ground. Kiowa and Comanche Indians roamed the region of Texas a mere 100 years ago.

People from all walks of life throughout the country saw Route 66 as a ticket to a new and better life "out West." During the late 1940s and into the 1950s families took to the road for their yearly vacations, often heading through Texas, which was fine as far as Texans were concerned. Route 66, which arrived in Texas in 1926, played an integral role in the economic growth of towns like Shamrock, McLean, Groom, Amarillo, Vega, and Adrain.

Early on, a journey through Texas on Route 66 was a rough, bumpy, and often hazardous ride. Because the Texas Highway Department gave priority to roads serving cities like Dallas, Houston, and San Antonio, conditions on 66 were generally subpar. One case in point was the dreaded "Jericho Gap," the portion stretching between McLean and Groom. After a rainfall many locals made extra cash by pulling stranded motorists out of the thick mud with teams of horses. In 1932 the section from McLean to Alanreed was bypassed and paved leaving about 18 miles of dirt from Alanreed to Groom. In 1933 construction finally began on a paved bypass there as well, but it wasn't until 1937 that the work was completed, making the stretch that paralleled the dreaded Jericho Gap one of the last sections on all of Route 66 to be paved.

During World War II military truck traffic took its toll on Route 66 in Texas, as it did in Missouri, and the surge of postwar automobile traffic further deteriorated the roadbed. Nevertheless, postwar families braved the road by the scores. Unlike its role in the 1920s and 1930s, Texas became a frontrunner in highway safety in the years following the war. Jack Rittenhouse, author of *A Guide Book to Highway 66* (1946), wrote when crossing the border from Oklahoma, "At once the road improves. Texas has wide splendid roads with excellent shoulders. There are many roadside parks throughout this part of the state." By 1954 Highway 66 was a modern four-lane highway from the Oklahoma border to just east of Groom, and from Amarillo west to Bushland. All of Route 66 in Texas was upgraded to four-lane status by 1960, with Interstate 40 designation from Shamrock to Conway. By 1966 the only two-lane section still in use was east of Vega to Glenrio at the New Mexico border. By the mid-1970s I-40 bypassed most Texas towns, with the exceptions of McLean and Groom. Amarillo, the largest Route 66 city in Texas, was completely bypassed in 1968. Groom survived the interstate until 1980, and McLean, one of the last holdouts along the entire route, did not succumb to I-40 until 1984.

Many of the towns that once enjoyed the abundance of postwar tourist travel have suffered the same sad fate as the road itself. During the road's heyday a trip west through Texas would include a multitude of "tourist traps." Live rattlesnake pits and great gas prices were but a few of the marketing ploys designed to convince travelers to stop. Some still exist but most have gone the way of the dial telephone. One holdover is the Big Texan Steak Ranch in Amarillo, which has a standing offer: finish their 72-ounce steak with all of the fixins' in one hour, and the meal is free.

U DROP INN, SHAMROCK
c. 1942

The art deco U Drop Inn at the intersection of Route 66 and U.S Highway 83 was built in 1936 from plans scratched out in the dirt by John Nunn with an old nail. So the story goes. The main building was built of brick with green and gold glazed tile accents, while the towers are wood-framed and covered with stucco. A contest to name the café was won by a local 10-year-old who pocketed $5 in the process. As the only café for about a 100-mile radius, the U Drop Inn enjoyed a brisk business.

Around 1937 the space next to the café that served as a store was transformed into a dining room and ballroom. Original proprietors John and Bebe Nunn sold the café after a few years, only to repurchase it in 1950 and change its name to Nunn's Café. John died in 1957, and in 1960 Bebe sold the business to Grace Brunner, who changed the name once again. The rechristened Tower Café also served as Shamrock's Greyhound bus station and fed hundreds of travelers daily. After a few more ownership changes, the building was purchased in the early 1980s by the son of the original financier, James Tindal Jr., who had the building repainted to its original color and restored the U Drop Inn moniker. Today the U Drop Inn is an information center created with a $1.7 million federal restoration grant.

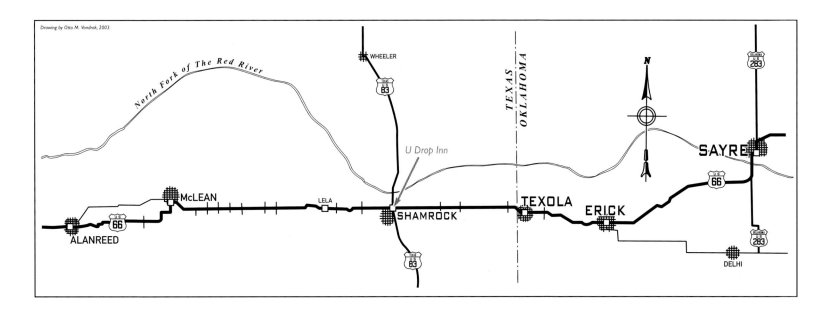

Drawing by Otto M. Vondrak, 2003.

AMARILLO
c. 1958

In 1887 the Fort Worth & Denver City Railway was building across the Texas panhandle when it established a tent city, known as "Ragtown," along an area creek. A permanent townsite was subsequently argued over and voted on. On August 30, 1887, the site proposed by local rancher Colonel James T. Berry was selected. Originally called Oneida, it was soon changed to Amarillo (Spanish for "yellow"), some say for the color of the soil along the creek banks, others for the region's abundant yellow wildflowers. By 1893 it was said that Amarillo's population was "between 500-600 humans and 50,000 head of cattle."

In the early days, Route 66 entered Amarillo from the east via Northeast 8th Street (now Amarillo Boulevard) and continued just north of downtown, where it took a 90-degree turn south on Fillmore Street. The highway traveled through downtown, west on 6th Street, and on through San Jacinto Heights, veering off to 9th Street and eventually out of the city. Route 66 on 8th Street at the eastern end of town was considered "motel row," where dozens of tourist courts lined the street with colorful names like the Cowboy Motel, Cactus Motel, Silver Spur, Longhorn, and Wagon Wheel. By 1953 traffic was rerouted west on Amarillo Boulevard past Fillmore Street to relieve the traffic snarl downtown. The San Jacinto portion was paved in brick in 1927, making it the first paved highway in Amarillo. In 1968 Interstate 40 opened to traffic, bypassing the city and motel row.

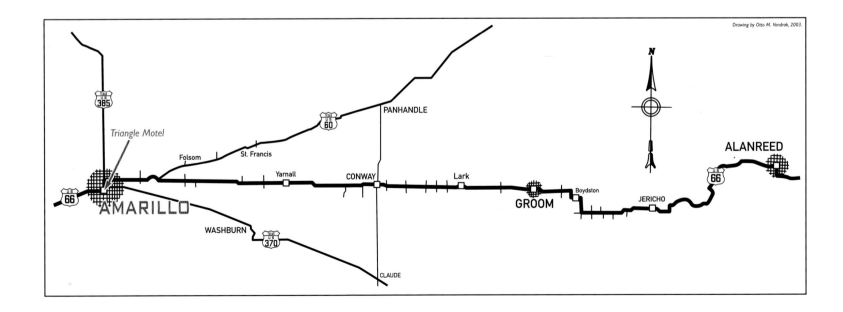

Drawing by Otto M. Vondrak, 2003.

TRIANGLE MOTEL, AMARILLO
c. 1949

S. M. Clayton was onetime mayor of Borger, Texas, known among some as "the wickedest town in the West." After his retirement from politics he and his wife Cora moved to Amarillo and built the Triangle Motel complex on the eastern edge of town, naming it for its wedge-shaped lot created by the intersection of Route 66 and Highway 60. The streamline moderne motel was designed with two parallel brick buildings that faced each other, separated by a courtyard in the center. Each building housed six rooms and a convenient, closed-in two-car garage between every two rooms.

During its heyday, the Triangle catered to the families and dependants of servicemen stationed at the nearby Lackland Air Force Base. In the late 1950s the Strategic Air Command opened the 4128th Strategic Wing at the base and extended its runways to accommodate the newer and bigger jets. Highway 60 was closed as a result. In 1968 the motel suffered two major setbacks with the deactivation of the air base and the completion of the Interstate bypass around Amarillo. Slowly, the motel fell into a state of disrepair. In 1977 Vaughn and Ramona Price bought the property and used the empty buildings mostly for storage. The structure that once housed the restaurant has since been opened and now serves as a bar and local hangout.

VEGA MOTEL, VEGA
c. 1960

In the small town of Vega, 40 miles west of Amarillo, sits the Vega Motel at the crossroads of old Route 66 and U.S. 385. E. M. and Josephine Pancoast built the 20-unit motel in the early 1940s, and it is a prime example of the era's U-shaped motor courts with a fully covered garage for each unit and a central courtyard. The property was sold to Ethridge Betts in the early 1970s, and the current owners, Harold and Tresa Whaley, bought the motel in 1988. Tresa sews the bedspreads and curtains used in the rooms. Many of the rooms have been remodeled, but Tresa says they are careful not to ruin the old charm and style. "Love, sweat and tears have gone into this place,"

says Tresa. When a blizzard left guests snowbound in 1991, Tresa's brother Manuel and daughter Joanna trekked to the grocery store in a four-wheel-drive vehicle. Tresa and Joanna then fixed a traditional Thanksgiving dinner for her family and stranded guests.

Unlike many owners of motels from this era, the Whaleys have not converted the garages to rooms, thus maintaining the 1940s styling. At the time of this writing, paperwork had begun to add the motel to the National Register of Historic Places. Tresa speaks fondly of the fact that in the early 1990s country music star Vince Gill shot the video for his song "I Never Knew Lonely" in Room 21.

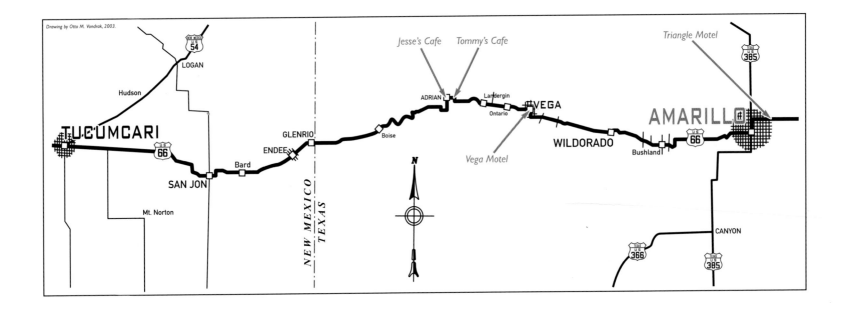

Drawing by Otto M. Vondrak, 2003.

TOMMY'S CAFÉ, ADRIAN
c. 1962

Manuel Loveless built the Kozy Kottage Kamp in Adrian in the early 1940s. The Kamp's service station and café were destroyed by fire in December 1947, but the Loveless family continued renting cabins under the name Adrian Court. The property where the service station and café once stood was sold to the Harris family. Bob Harris, who had worked at the Kozy Kottage Kamp before World War II, returned after the war with the idea of building a café on the newly acquired property. Harris wanted to design the café in a way that would compel motorists to stop. The nearby U.S. Army Air Force bases were selling surplus military items, including a control tower. Harris bought the tower, moved it to his property, and proceeded to build his café around it. The eatery was christened the Bent Door Café for the canted door that accommodated its slanting walls.

Harris left Adrian and his mother to operate the café, and in 1950 Loveless leased the restaurant. In the late 1960s the Interstate bypassed Adrian and the steady flow of traffic slowed to a trickle. In 1970 the onetime 24-hour café and service station closed their doors. They sat empty for three decades until Harris returned for a visit and heard the café was to be condemned. He repurchased the property and set a reopening for September 9, 1995, but it wasn't to be. On September 9 the fryers and ovens sat empty and cold. The café has remained closed since.

JESSE'S CAFÉ, ADRIAN
c. 1965

In 1956 Dub Edmonds and former Navy cook Jesse Fincher opened Jesse's Café in "an old building a cowboy built of cinder blocks," recalls Edmonds. A gas station located alongside the café was also part of their enterprise, which at one time was a one-room, dirt-floor café called Zella's. In 1965 a second story A-frame apartment was added above the café and a new canopy was built over the pumps. The apartment burned twice and was not rebuilt after the second fire. Jesse's Café was so successful that a second restaurant, Jesse's #2, went up in nearby Wilderado about 30 miles east of Adrian. Edmonds and Fincher ran both locations until 1976 when they sold the Adrian location to Terry and Peggy Crietz, who changed the name to Peggy's. The business was later sold again and became known as Rachel's.

Fincher's pies became famous in Adrian. Dub remembers, "He would bake pies and set them on the counter and most of them were sold before they got cold." Fincher passed away in 1989, leaving business matters to Edmonds, who sold the Wilderado location in 1991. Fran Hauser bought the Adrian location in 1990 and changed the name to the Adrian Café. Around 1995 she learned that Adrian was the mid-point on Route 66 and changed the name to the Mid-Point Café. Hauser continues the fine tradition of good food, friendly service, and delicious homemade pies begun in 1956.

NEW MEXICO

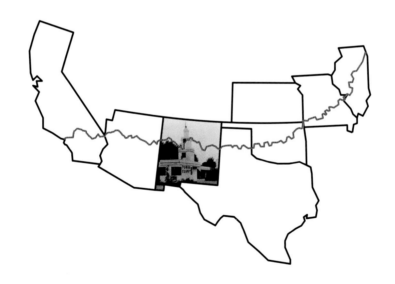

New Mexico was only 14 years old when Route 66 was created. The original 506-mile alignment through the state traversed many difficult obstacles, including deserts, snake-like canyons, and treacherous hills. Often the route utilized portions of the century-old Santa Fe Trail and the 300-year-old Camino Réal. The original alignment between Albuquerque and Santa Fe was considered the most treacherous and included the feared La Bajada Hill (Spanish for "the descent"). From 1926 to 1932 the hill provided early motorists with a multitude of challenges, including an average 6 percent grade and 20 switchbacks in 1.4 miles. Prior to the addition of fuel pumps in automobiles, motorists often climbed the hill in reverse to keep fuel flowing to gravity-fed carburetors. Descending La Bajada presented its own dangers. Early brake pads were often made of cloth and not very durable—riding one's brakes down the grade often set the pads on fire. At the top of the hill the State Highway Department posted a warning sign that read, "La Bajada Hill – Warning – Safe Speed 10 Mile – Watch Sharp Curves – This Road Is Not Fool Proof But Safe For A Sane Driver – Use Low Gear."

As automobiles gained popularity, many of the older paths traveled by Highway 66 quickly became obsolete. New Mexico saw its fair share of realignments, none as dramatic as that which took place in 1926. Around that time, Arthur T. Hannet was losing his bid for reelection as governor in a closely fought race. Feeling betrayed by his own political party and frustrated with state politics Hannet decided to avenge his loss by building a highway that would bypass the state capital. Governor-elect Richard Dillon would be sworn in in less than two months, so Hannet had little time to act. He called on state highway engineer E. B. Bail to begin a road-building project to start 6 miles west of Santa Rosa and head straight into Albuquerque. At the time, Highway 66 through New Mexico ran from Tucumcari to Santa Rosa, then to Romeroville, Glorieta, Santa Fe, and Albuquerque. Hannet's road would shorten the route to Albuquerque by about 89 miles and bypass Santa Fe's business community and politicians. By the time crews and equipment were secured, only 31 days remained to build 69 miles of roadway.

Angry citizens on Highway 66 to the north and Highway 60 to the south often sabotaged equipment, afraid of the economic impact of the new route. Vandalism, along with bitterly cold weather, slowed progress, but work forged ahead. Bail even brought the men blankets so they could sleep close to the machinery and protect it from further damage. Although the men worked non-stop, the new road was not quite finished by January 1. Dillon, immediately after taking oath on January 1, sent a representative to halt the construction. Bad weather kept him from arriving until January 3, however, by which time the road was completed. Hannet had his revenge. His road was originally designated New Mexico 6, paved by 1937, and redesignated as Highway 66 that same year.

The last segment of Route 66 in New Mexico was bypassed in 1981, four years before the entire route was officially decommissioned. In 1994 the surviving sections of Route 66 in New Mexico were designated as State Scenic Byways and in 2000 were recognized as National Scenic Byways.

TUCUMCARI
c. 1957

Tucumcari (pronounced *too-come-carry*) was first christened Six Gun Siding, but in 1902 citizens agreed that a more "respectful" name was needed, so they named it after a nearby mountain. Legend has it that a chief ordered two competing braves to the top of the mountain to fight to the death for the honor of marrying his daughter, Kari. Her lover, Tocom, lost the battle and in a violent rage she killed the victorious brave. Filled with anguish, she then sunk Tocom's knife into her own heart. Upon seeing what had transpired, the chief took the knife and plunged it into his own heart. Use your imagination, adjust the spelling a little, and voila.

During the halcyon days of Route 66, the indelible words "Tucumcari Tonight! 2,000 Motel Rooms" were splattered across billboards from Oklahoma City to California. Tucumcari was known as the town that was "two blocks wide and two miles long," for the concentration of motels, service stations, trading posts, and cafés along Route 66 through town. In the early days, however, Route 66 from the Texas border to Tucumcari was not well maintained and extremely narrow. Old timers would remark that you had "six inches and a cigarette paper between you and death on 66." Interstate 40 bypassed Tucumcari in 1980, but the town managed to survive. There may be fewer motel rooms these days, but the main drag is still filled with historic Route 66 motels, cafés, trading posts, and a legend or two for good measure.

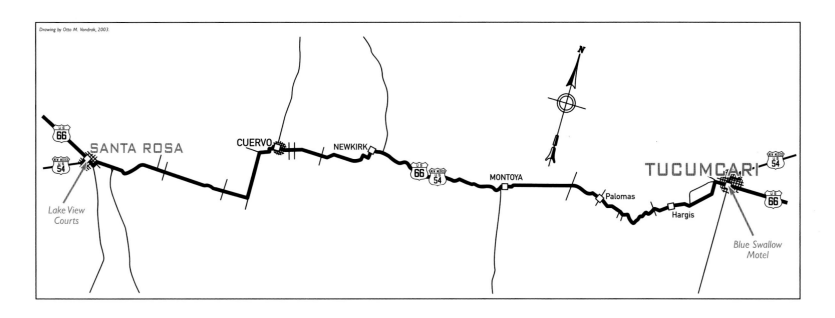

Drawing by Otto M. Vondrak, 2003.

BLUE SWALLOW COURT, TUCUMCARI, NEW MEXICO

In the City, East on U. S. Highway 66

BLUE SWALLOW COURT, TUCUMCARI
c. 1941

Since the early 1940s, the Blue Swallow has been a favorite haven among weary travelers. W. A. Huggins began construction on this truly classic motor court in 1939 and opened for business in 1941. The archetypal 1930s design features 13 units laid out in an L-shape with individual garages for each unit. The office sits prominently in the center. Ownership changed hands a few times over the years until 1958 when Floyd Redman purchased the property and gave it to his fiancée as an engagement gift. Lillian Redman owned and operated the motel for almost 40 years until age and the high cost of upkeep took their toll.

Slowly, the motel was headed downhill from lack of maintenance and Redman was forced to put it up for sale. With no prospective buyers it seemed another Route 66 icon was about to fade away. Fortunately, Dale and Linda Bakke saw an ad in a Denver newspaper listing the Blue Swallow for sale and, looking for a change of scenery, purchased the property. On March 13, 1998, substantial restoration efforts began. Unit by unit, room by room, and fixture by fixture, the classic Blue Swallow was lifted from the brink of extinction. Lillian Redman passed away in February of 1999 but no doubt would smile as once again the Blue Swallow proudly serves tired travelers.

SANTA ROSA
c. 1958

Santa Rosa, was founded in 1865 when rancher Don Celso Baca, drawn by the abundance of water, arrived and became "lord of the region" under the old custom of range domain. He named the new settlement after his wife and Saint Rose of Lima, the first canonized saint of the so-called New World. The coming of the railroad on Christmas Day 1901 turned the sleepy settlement into a vital transportation and service hub. Ironically, water, which attracted the railroad, was also the reason that industry fled Santa Rosa: the water was so high in mineral content it left gypsum deposits in steam engines, ruining the locomotives. With the departure of the railroad, Santa Rosa reverted to the sleepy town it once was.

When Highway 66 was routed through in 1926, Santa Rosa became an important stop. At one time, as many as 60 service stations, 20 motels, and 15 restaurants lined its main thoroughfare. The famous Blue Hole, located on one of Route 66's early alignments through town, is a natural, bell-shaped pool over 80 feet deep with amazing clarity and a constant water temperature of 64 degrees Fahrenheit. Scuba divers from around the country enjoy its unique blue waters. During the Dust Bowl era, the Blue Hole and the surrounding area served as a campground for thousands of migrants.

LAKE VIEW COURTS, SANTA ROSA
c. 1946

The Lake View Courts were built in 1941 and consisted of 10 units with covered garage parking for four of the rooms. A station serving Conoco gas was also part of the original structure. The motel operated as a successful business for 20 years until the early 1960s when the owner allowed it to fall into a state of disrepair. In the mid-1960s Canuto Sanchez Jr. purchased the property with the intent of tearing the motel down and erecting a new modern Ramada Inn in its place. Canuto decided against the new motel when news that the impending Interstate would eventually bypass Santa Rosa was confirmed. He opted to spruce up the existing motel with some fresh paint and to furnish the rooms with new beds and furniture. Along with the new look came a new name and the Lake View Courts were changed to the Plains Motel. The newly remodeled inn and newly added Amoco gas station became favorite stops in town until November 1972 when the Interstate was completed, leaving Santa Rosa high and dry. The motel closed in April 1973 and has been used for storage for the past 30 years. The service station reopened in 1975 under the Exxon banner and remained open until 1980.

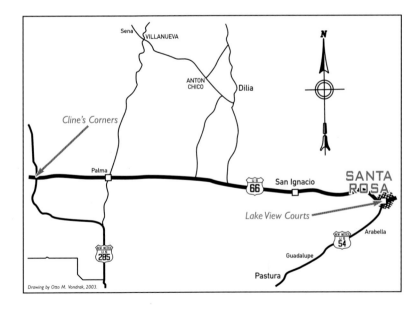

Drawing by Otto M. Vondrak, 2003.

LAKE VIEW COURTS
STATION-CAFE-MODERN COTTAGES
SANTA ROSA, N. MEX.

CLINE'S CORNERS
c. 1958

After several failed business ventures in New Mexico and Arkansas, Roy Cline and his son Roy Jr. in 1934 leased 80 acres where Highways 6 and 2 intersected and built a small café and Conoco station. In 1937 the highways were paved and relocated, so Roy had the buildings jacked up and moved to the new intersection, Highway 2 now being U.S. Highway 285 and Highway 6 becoming Route 66. During the early years, things were tough going. At night Roy turned on the lights only when a car approached. If they stopped he left them on; if they passed, he turned them off and waited for another car.

Eventually, Cline's Corners became Roy's most lucrative venture. He sold the business in 1939 and moved, but eventually returned to New Mexico and opened another Route 66 service station, which he owned and operated until 1963. Located 77 miles east of Albuquerque, the Flying C Ranch at first consisted of a gas station, garage, and café. Today, it is a fully modern facility known as Bowlin's Flying C Ranch, and includes a gas station, curio shop, and Dairy Queen. After Roy sold Cline's Corners, it became so large that in 1964 a post office was added and homes were built behind the business to provide living quarters for most of its 48 employees. Over the years Cline's Corners became a Route 66 landmark and, later, a favorite stop on Interstate 40 that today serves an estimated 15 million customers each year.

LONGHORN RANCH, MORIARTY
c. 1948

"Where the West Stops to Rest" was the catchy advertising slogan of the Longhorn Ranch. Located 45 miles east of Albuquerque, the Longhorn sat along Route 66 on the barren desert landscape of eastern New Mexico, tempting first-time travelers out West to stop and rest a spell. "Captain Eric" Erikson, a former police officer from back East, opened the Longhorn with only a counter and a few stools. Eventually the tiny café was expanded to include a restaurant, coffee shop, cocktail lounge, motel, curio shop, and full-service garage. The storefronts were set up to look like the Western towns one would see in the movies, with a pair of totem poles guarding the curio shop.

The Longhorn was the first taste of the Old West for many motorists traveling along Route 66. Among the many attractions at the ranch, riding the bright red stagecoach, pulled by four paint horses with Hondo the Cowboy at the reins, was probably the most popular. Afterward, kids could have their picture taken with Hondo and the stagecoach. The Longhorn Ranch also kept several exotic animals on display for tourists to enjoy, including oxen, a large Brahma bull, buffalo, and a special longhorn steer named "Babe." The Longhorn Ranch became a landmark institution on Route 66, and at its height of popularity hosted thousands of tourists each day. Today, only ruins and memories remain of one of the most glamorous tourist attractions on Route 66.

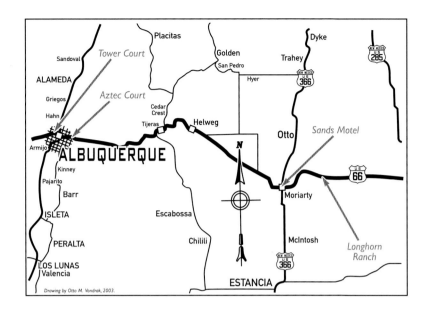

Tower Court

Aztec Court

Sands Motel

Longhorn Ranch

Drawing by Otto M. Vondrak, 2003.

SANDS MOTEL, MORIARTY
c. 1954

A man today remembered as Mr. Simms built the Sands Motel in 1954 to consist of six rooms with enclosed garages alongside each room. As with many Route 66 motor courts, the garages were eventually converted to four rooms. Simms owned the motel for a very short time, selling the property in 1955. In 1968, J. C. Alderson, a plumber by trade, bought the property and eventually expanded the room total to 18 by adding two trailers out back for extra rooms. A trucking company with a regular route through Moriarty used the trailer rooms.

"We never had much trouble around here except one day around 1972," recalls Alderson's son, Jace. "One morning we went in to clean one of the rooms that was rented by a couple the night before and found the sheets, pillowcases, blankets, towels, and TV missing. That night our next-door neighbor, who owned a wrecker service, pulled in with a wrecked car. I asked what happened and he said, 'Someone stole [the] car last night . . . if you look in the backseat I think that there are some things in there that belong to you.' Sure enough, all of our missing items were in the backseat. It turns out the couple was on the run and wanted by the FBI." The Aldersons rented nightly rooms until they sold the property in 2001. At the time of this writing, the motel was being remodeled for use as storefronts.

AZTEC COURT, ALBUQUERQUE
c. 1941

In 1931 Guy and May Fargo built the Aztec Court at an estimated cost of $8,000 at 3821 Central Avenue on the east side of Albuquerque. "Innerspring mattresses, furnace heat and moderate rates" were some of the advertised amenities. In 1937 Route 66 was relocated to New Mexico 6, a straight shot from Santa Rosa to Albuquerque, giving Central Avenue a major increase in traffic. Tourist-based businesses began popping up all along the street, as a steady stream of automobiles flowed down Route 66, especially in the summer months. Guy passed away in 1942 but May continued to operate the motel until she sold it in 1944. Two years later the property was again sold to a pair of couples, William and Emma Geck and Wesley and Bertha Meyer, who owned and operated the motel until the early 1950s. Later in the decade the name was changed several more times through the course of eight ownership changes. In 1958 Floyd and Evelyn Lewis bought the property and changed the name to Aztec Motel, which remains in use today. The Aztec passed through a few more hands between 1962 and 1992, when Mohamed and Shokey Natha bought the property. After 64 years and 14 ownership changes, the oldest continuously operated auto court on New Mexico's Route 66 was entered into the National Register of Historic Places in 1993.

TOWER COURT, ALBUQUERQUE
c. 1939

The Tower Court was built by Ben F. Shear in 1939, just two years after the relocation of Route 66 through Albuquerque via Central Avenue. The mostly single-story motel was constructed using the classic U-shape layout and utilizes a distinctively streamline moderne architectural style. Typical of auto court design during the 1930s, pull-in garages were located alongside each unit, with all but one still in use today. The unusual rear wing of the motel contains a second story consisting of two units mirroring the lower units. Originally, a 30-foot stepped tower containing the motel office was located at the front of the property, accentuating the unique design of the motel. The tower has since been removed. The motel was originally built containing 15 units and remained that way with no additions over its lifetime. The Tower Court was a member of the United Auto Courts and was a recommended stop by AAA. Eventually, to keep up with the times, the "Court" was dropped and the name was changed to the Tower Motel. Relatively unchanged since 1939, the Tower Motel is one of the oldest remaining tourist courts along Albuquerque's Central Avenue/Route 66 commercial strip. It is also a classic example of auto courts built prior to World War II. The Tower Motel no longer serves nightly guests but is an apartment building renting units by the month. On November 22, 1993, it was added to the National Register of Historic Places.

JOHNNIES CAFÉ, THOREAU
C. LATE 1920s

At the time of its construction, both Johnnies and Highway 66, then a primitive dirt path, were located on the north side of the tracks in Thoreau (pronounced *thuh-roo*). In February 1936, founders Johnnie and Helen Maich sold the business to John and Anna Radosevich. John was the cook and his wife Anna did a little bit of everything, including waiting tables. The small café was only 20x40 and consisted of a counter with a couple of stools and four tables. In its early years, the food was prepared on a Coleman wood stove and dishes were washed with water heated by a wood fire. A one-cylinder diesel generator was pressed into service to supply electricity for lights during the evening hours. Shortly after John and Anna purchased the café, Route 66 was rerouted to the south side of the tracks. Johnnies itself was moved, building and all, to its current location along side the new alignment in 1947. In 1949 an addition was made to the building's east side, and in the early 1950s another section was built on to the west side. Today, the western addition is an off-sale liquor store. Johnnies was well known in the area for serving outstanding chili and thick steaks. "People would drive from Gallup just for the chili," says John Radosevich, whose family still owns the building.

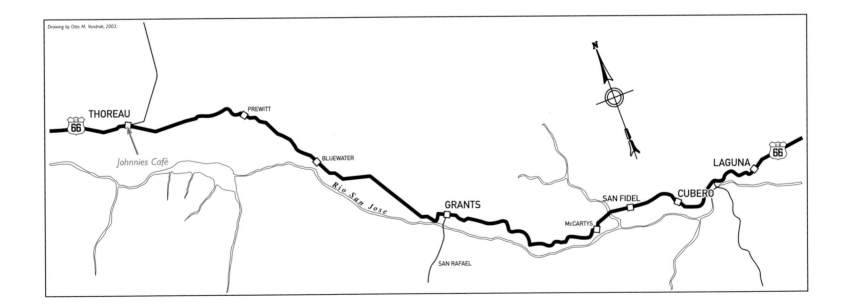

Drawing by Otto M. Vondrak, 2003.

JOHNNIES CAFE, THOREAU, N. MEX.
GOOD EATS
Reasonable Prices   Tourist Headquarters
U. S. HIGHWAY 66

Mileage from Johnnies Cafe

WEST TO		EAST TO	
Continental Divide	5	Grants	31
Gallup, N. Mexico	32	Laguna	65
Painted Desert	196	Los Lunas	116
Petrified Forest	118	Albuquerque	139
Holbrook, Ariz.	134	Domingo	176
Winslow	167	Santa Fe	203
Flagstaff	230	Las Vegas	277
Maine	250	Trinidad, Colo.	418
Grand Canyon	315	**NORTH TO**	
Williams	266	Crown Point	28
Needles, Cal.	470	Chaco Canyon	60
Los Angeles	770	**SOUTH TO**	
		Albuquerque	139
		El Paso	444

LOG CABIN LODGE, GALLUP
c. 1952

Tony and Francis Leone built the Log Cabin Lodge in 1937. Originally, it consisted of six log cabins and a single-story office building. A fireplace in each cabin provided ambience and heat during the cold winter nights. "Every day, each cabin was set up with a supply of paper and logs for an evening fire" says Lois Berger, daughter of Tony and Francis. Each cabin also featured a kitchenette, all of which were eventually eliminated because of the added time required to clean up after guests. Beds replaced the kitchen appliances, adding extra sleeping space to each cabin. Navajo rugs and taxidermy filled the roomy lobby that also offered a large central fireplace.

During the 1940s and 1950s the Log Cabin Lodge was part of the Best Western chain and two double log cabins were added, as well as a whole new wing built in an adobe style with side-by-side rooms and attached garages. The property was sold around 1959, but the new owner was unable to keep up with the mortgage payments and the lodge reverted back to the Leones. Multiple owners followed, but time took its toll on the landmark. Maintenance and upkeep over the years were sorely lacking and the Log Cabin Lodge eventually fell into a dismal state of disrepair. The Log Cabin Lodge was listed on the National Register of Historic Places in 1993. The last guest checked out sometime in the mid-1990s and it has remained vacant ever since.

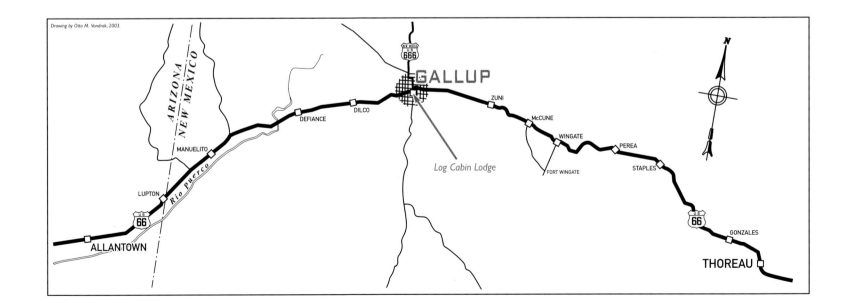

Drawing by Otto M. Vondrak, 2003.

Log Cabin Lodge

LOG CABIN LODGE
GALLUP, NEW MEXICO

U. S. Highway 66, ¼ Mile West of Business Center

ARIZONA

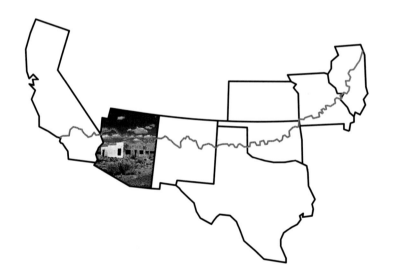

When U.S. Highway 66 was designated in 1926, existing roads, variations of Beale's Wagon Road and other old trails, were stitched together from town to town to form the fledgling highway. Highway 66 entered Arizona from the east via Lupton and continued through Holbrook, Winslow, Winona, Flagstaff, Williams, Ash Fork, Seligman, Peach Springs, Kingman, Oatman, and finally Topock.

U.S. Highway 66 originally spanned 385 miles across northern Arizona, and, as in other states, a vast majority of the road was dirt and poorly maintained. As traffic grew, motels, cafés, and service stations sprang up to accommodate travelers, and each town stretched its city limits as more and more businesses vied for the tourist dollar. By 1934 most of the Mother Road in Arizona was paved. Near the end of 1937 paving was complete across Arizona, which also saw its fair share of alignment changes over the years. In 1953 the perilous hairpin path from Kingman to Oatman over Sitgreaves Pass was eliminated in favor of a straighter route bypassing Oatman via Yucca on its way to Topock. In the May 1955 issue of *Arizona Highways* it was reported that 2,999 vehicles used Route 66 in Arizona every day, or 1,094,635 vehicles per year, of which 73 percent were from out of state. In 1955, the magazine added, the total length of Route 66 through Arizona was 376 miles, with 174.8 being constructed to the minimum 40-foot width, the Interstate standard.

Construction of Interstate 40 in Arizona was full speed ahead in the 1960s, and by 1969 most rural sections of Route 66 were upgraded or replaced. The first city to be bypassed was Flagstaff in 1968, but construction of other city bypasses moved at a much slower rate and it wasn't until 1978 that the next city, Winslow, saw a bypass. That same year the Interstate opened from Seligman to Kingman, leaving numerous small towns in an economic nosedive, including Peach Springs, which holds the dubious honor of being bypassed by 36 miles, the most of any city on the route. Holbrook, Joseph City, Ash Fork, and Kingman were all bypassed in 1981, but it wasn't until October 13, 1984, that Williams became the last city on the entire route to be bypassed.

Route 66 across Arizona is a study in scenic contrasts as one travels west from the wide-open spaces of the eastern high desert on a gradual climb through the beautiful, dense pine forests east of Flagstaff to Williams. From Williams, at an elevation of 7,000 feet, 66 drops abruptly down Ash Fork Hill to just over 5,000 feet in about 6 miles. From Ash Fork, the route travels west past Seligman, where the landscape changes again and the treeless expanse of the Aubrey Valley comes into view. From there, the road gradually descends over rolling hills to Kingman at 3,328 feet, eventually reaching the low desert terrain of Topock and the Colorado River, where the elevation is a mere 507 feet above sea level. Much of the Mother Road in Arizona lies directly beneath the path of Interstate 40. Nevertheless, there are still many sections of the old road that survive and are well worth the time to explore them.

PAINTED DESERT
TRADING POST, NAVAJO
c. 1942

Imagine the loneliest, most sun-baked desert expanse conceivable, where a single lizard might be the only living thing—other than yourself—for miles. There, right smack dab in the middle of lonely, you will find the Painted Desert Trading Post. Dotch and Alberta Windsor opened the Painted Desert Trading Post in the early 1940s, selling Indian curios, cold drinks, and sandwiches, as well as gasoline from gravity pumps. The trading post had no telephone, so calls were placed at the Painted Desert Park several miles to the west. Appliances ran on electricity generated by a windmill. The Windsors operated the post together until their marriage ended around 1950. Joy Nevin, who ran a veterinary supply business in Holbrook, Arizona,

met Dotch at the trading post during a business trip and the couple married, with Joy giving birth to a daughter in 1952. Dotch and Joy operated the trading post together until they divorced in 1956.

The section of Route 66 that ran past the business was relocated, widened, and designated Interstate 40 in the late 1950s, and the trading post has sat empty and abandoned ever since. Joy went on to become a leading figure in nearby Holbrook, where a street is named in her honor. Dotch died in October 1964, but the skeletal remains of the Painted Desert Trading Post still sit alongside the abandoned roadway, slowly being reclaimed by the desert that once gave it life.

116

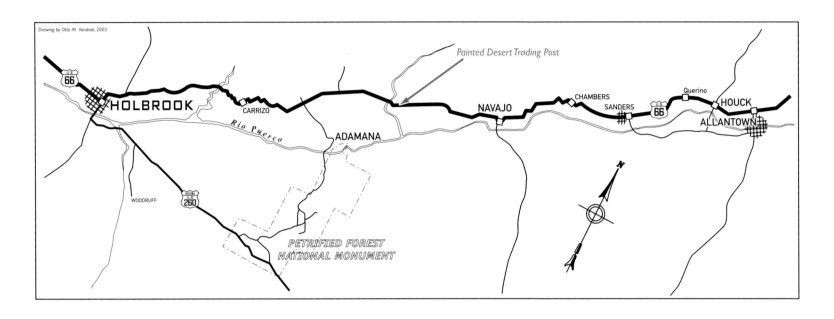

Drawing by Otto M. Vondrak, 2003.

Painted Desert Trading Post

HOLBROOK
CARRIZO
Rio Puerco
ADAMANA
WOODRUFF
PETRIFIED FOREST
NATIONAL MONUMENT
NAVAJO
CHAMBERS
SANDERS
Querino
HOUCK
ALLANTOWN

ELLA'S FRONTIER
TRADING POST, JOSEPH CITY
c. 1950s

Ella's Frontier Trading Post sits on an abandoned section of Route 66 just outside the western edge of Joseph City. The business was owned and operated by Ella Blackwell, who purchased the property (previously called the Last Frontier Trading Post) in 1955 after divorcing her second husband. A former student at the Julliard School, Ella kept a piano in the store, which she claimed was established in 1873, making it the oldest such establishment on Route 66. Ella, however, was considered quite eccentric among locals, many of whom doubted her claim. Nevertheless, Ella's Frontier was in every way a classic tourist stop. Most of the things sold there—feather headdresses, moccasins, rubber snakes—would be considered mere souvenirs to adults, but treasures to kids traveling out West with their folks. Theo Hunsaker, the executor of Ella's estate, claims, "She had acquaintances all over the world; people who had stopped there would stay in touch with her." When she died in 1984, Hunsaker found duffel bags full of her correspondence.

In 1969, Interstate 40 bypassed Ella's, marking the beginning of the end for the longstanding roadside tourist stop. Standing on the dead-end road that once carried hundreds of automobiles each day with travelers gazing at Ella's Frontier and dreaming of the cold soda in the machine door or the large tomahawk under the counter glass, you get the feeling of being in a life-size, historical diorama—a living museum piece complete with a barely audible Mozart sonata drifting through the ruins.

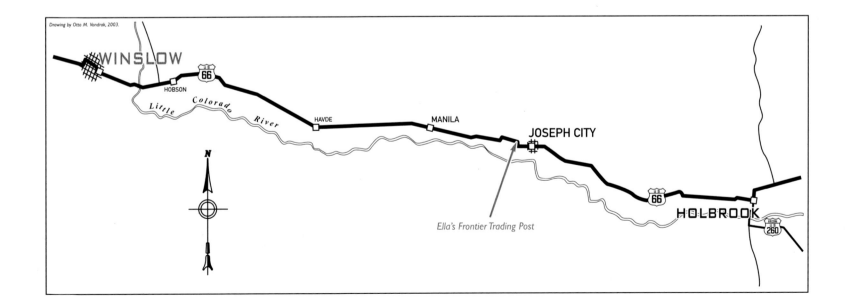

Drawing by Otto M. Vondrak, 2003.

Ella's Frontier Trading Post

WINSLOW
c. 1938

"Standin' on a corner in Winslow, Arizona/Such a fine sight to see." The popular Eagles song of the early 1970s immortalized the corner of Second Street and Kingsley in downtown Winslow. Second Street carried Route 66 until 1951, when the ever-increasing stream of cars made it necessary to divide the flow of traffic through town. Second Street was assigned one-way traffic eastbound, and Third Street carried westbound travelers. Unfortunately, this grizzled railroad town fell on hard times when Interstate 40 bypassed it in the late 1960s and most businesses moved out nearer to the Interstate, leaving downtown Winslow looking somewhat like a ghost town.

Signs along this portion of the route commemorate the stretch as being part of the old Beale's Wagon Road; other markers point out the use of this trail by Mormon immigrants in the 1870s. Wayne L. Troutner's Store for Men was the clothier of choice for locals and lonely travelers wanting to spruce up before "standin' on a corner" and hoping to be noticed by that special gal passing by in a "flatbed Ford." Like so many roadside business owners along Route 66, Troutner was innovative when it came to roadside advertising, and created quite a stir when he placed billboards depicting a vivacious young cowgirl along Route 66 and other highways out West. The billboards became popular worldwide with sightings reported as far away as Paris and Guam.

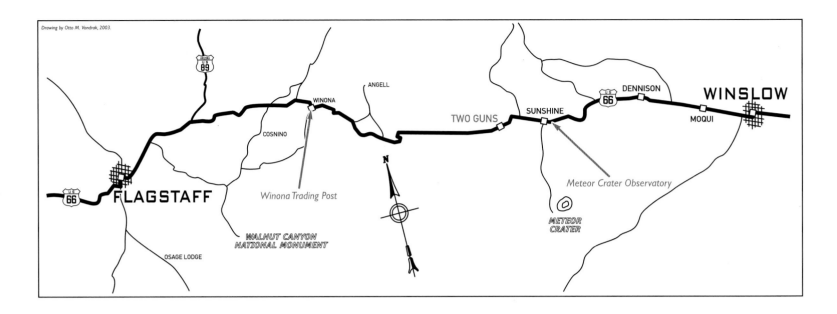

Drawing by Otto M. Vondrak, 2003.

METEOR CRATER OBSERVATORY, WEST OF WINSLOW
c. 1946

Harry and Hope Locke began work on the impressive, castle-like Meteor Crater Observatory structure in the mid-1930s. Despite Hope's passing, Harry continued work on the building, and in the late 1930s finally opened the observatory to the public. A few years later, the Meteor Crater Observatory closed its doors due to lack of visitors and the large debt accrued during its construction. Then, in 1946, Dr. Harvey H. Nininger leased the building and on October 19 opened the doors once again. Inspired by a meteor he saw while teaching in Kansas in 1923, Dr. Nininger dedicated his life to the study of hurtling space debris and is known as the founder of the scientific study of meteorites.

The crater itself was located about 6 miles south of the observatory. Visitors climbed the dark and very narrow stairs of the tower and waited their turn at the telescope—all for only 25 cents! The museum also housed concessions, meteorite samples, and a detailed model showing the path Arizona's meteor took as it sailed through the earth's atmosphere, eventually crashing to the desert floor. A few years after its reopening the facility became officially known as the American Meteorite Museum. Visible for many miles, it must have been a remarkable site. Even today the ruins can be seen out in the distance on Interstate 40, beckoning to passing cars. The Meteorite Museum hosted its last stargazer in 1953. Dr. Nininger died in 1986.

CORNER IN AMERICAN METEORITE MUSEUM
OPPOSITE METEOR CRATER HIGHWAY 66 IN ARIZONA

TWO GUNS
c. 1948

Located halfway between Winslow and Flagstaff, no other town on Route 66 has such a frightening and storied past. In 1881, the story goes, more than 50 Navajo men, women, and children were slaughtered by a band of Apaches at a Navajo camp in the nearby Painted Desert. Navajo warriors tracked the Apaches, trapped them in a nearby cave, and quickly gathered sagebrush, wood, and anything else that would burn. The Navajos then built a fire at the entrance to the cave, which quickly filled with fire and smoke, then opened fire into the cave. They entered it the next day to find the charred and riddled remains of 42 Apaches. The cave is still known as the Apache Death Cave and carries with it a curse of bad luck to anyone who enters or disturbs the site. Other legends include rumors of loot left in a nearby canyon by train robbers .

By the 1950s, Two Guns had become a very popular stop along Route 66. What kid wouldn't want to see the Indian cliff dwellings, mountain lions, and the occasional cowboy or Indian? Stores, cafés, a service station, and a motel were also there for tired tourists. The concrete bridge through town crosses the Canyon Diablo and was listed on the National Register of Historic Places in 1988. The former roadside stop is now a crumbling ghost town. Stop and visit at your own risk.

WINONA TRADING POST, WINONA
c. 1955

In the early 1920s Billy Adams built a one-story rock structure from river stones and nearby Indian ruins and called it the Winona Trading Post. He offered necessities for modern motorists, including fan belts, coils, tools, and tires. Cold drinks and dry goods were also available. In 1924 a post office was established in the trading post, and Myrtle Adams became the first female postmaster in Arizona. Soon after completing the trading post, Billy Adams and his sons built 10 small wooden cabins, said to comprise one of the first motor courts in the United States. Each cabin measured 10x14 and featured a wood-burning stove, mirror, and washstand. In 1925, Adams built the two-story Winona Motel, once again of stone. The motel had 14 rooms upstairs and a small lobby below. Through the 1940s it was a beehive of activity, especially during World War II when convoys of troops would come through town. Billy's son Ralph recalls, "They would buy every bottle of pop and every candy bar we had and run us out completely in one visit."

The early 1950s saw a realignment of Route 66 to its current location, and a new trading post, including a cafe, tourist cabins, and service station, was built alongside the new alignment. Billy Adams and his family eventually left the post to become ranchers. The current owners bulldozed the motel, trading post, and campground.

WILLIAMS

c. 1940s

Founded in 1876, Williams was named for the famed mountaineer William Sherley Williams. The railroad officially arrived in town in 1882, and Williams quickly grew into a lumber and ranching center. In 1901, the Santa Fe Railway built a 60-mile spur to the Grand Canyon, and Williams has since been known as the "Gateway to the Grand Canyon." By the turn of the century, Williams, like many western railroad towns, had a rough-and-tumble reputation, its streets lined with brothels, saloons, opium dens, and gambling houses. One would be hard pressed to find any evidence of that reputation today. This quaint, small town has changed little since Route 66 carried the masses west and grape Nehi was the drink of the day. One can walk the streets, lined with many fine motels and cafés, and feel magically transported to a different time, when life's hectic pace was a crawl compared to today. All this thanks largely to the fact that Williams (nicknamed "Little Las Vegas" in late 1930s for its abundant neon signage) holds the honor of being the last bypassed town on Route 66; the final 6 miles of Interstate 40 bypassed the town on October 13, 1984. That same year, the Downtown Business District of Williams was placed on the National Register of Historic Places. The population, holding at about 3,000, has not changed much in 60 years—no doubt the residents like it that way.

BILL WILLIAMS AVENUE

Looking East

WILLIAMS ARIZONA

X703

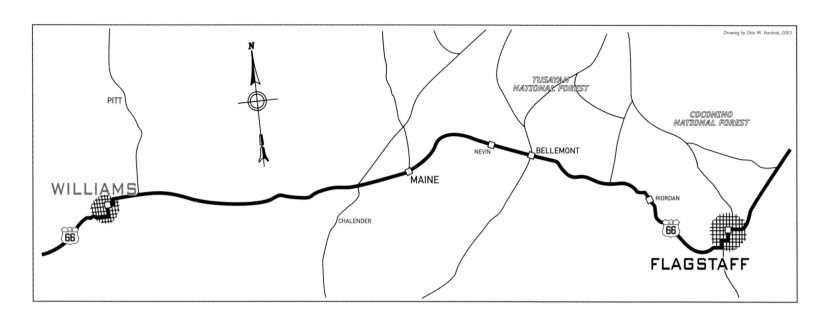

Drawing by Otto M. Vondrak, 2003.

U. S. HIGHWAY 66, EASTBOUND THROUGH
ASH FORK, ARIZONA

ASH FORK
c. 1948

In 1882 the Atlantic & Pacific Railway (later merged into the Santa Fe Railway) chose for a siding stop in the area now known as Ash Fork, named for the ash trees growing at the fork of nearby Ash Creek. The Ash Fork Livestock Company drove their cattle to the railhead, then shipped the animals east by rail. The cattle business—and the town—flourished. In 1893 Ash Fork was completely decimated by a fire, but was rebuilt and relocated to the other side of the tracks, where it still stands today.

A onetime hotbed of tourist activity, Ash Fork is today a shadow of its former self. The legendary Escalante, an elegant Harvey House hotel, was built along the Santa Fe tracks in 1907 and provided rail travelers fine dining and accommodations. In Route 66's heyday, dozens of motels, cafés, and gas stations lined the streets, offering much-needed services for travelers and vacationers. During World War II, regular troop trains brought thousands of servicepersons who eagerly spent their money there. When the Santa Fe moved its mainline 10 miles north of town in the 1950s, it marked the beginning of the end for the prosperous community. A fire destroyed many buildings in the early 1970s, and when the Interstate bypassed Ash Fork in 1979, the good times came to a screeching halt. Ash Fork, today known as the "Flagstone Capital of the U.S.A.," now sits quietly, waiting for the occasional stranded or hungry tourist.

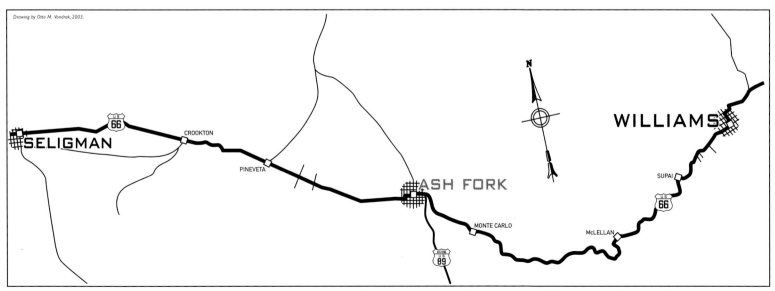

Drawing by Otto M. Vondrak, 2003.

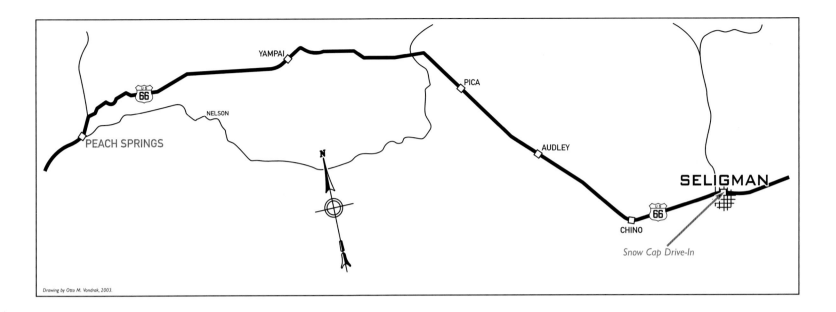

Drawing by Otto M. Vondrak, 2003.

Snow Cap Drive-In

SNOW CAP DRIVE-IN, SELIGMAN
c. 1953

Juan Delgadillo, with help from his father, built the landmark Snow Cap in 1953. A Santa Fe employee at the time, Juan used materials discarded by the railroad, earning the nickname the "Santa Fe Pack Rat." Juan at first sought to become part of the Dairy Queen network, but was turned down, so he searched for other companies to affiliate with, eventually settling on the Snow Cap Corporation of Prescott, Arizona. Snow Cap folded, but Delgadillo kept the name.

"The Snow Cap has its own life, its own humor," says son Robert Delgadillo, who works at the restaurant alongside Juan, his brother John, and sister Cecilia. Upon entering the Snow Cap, be careful not to grab the fake door handle attached to the hinged side of the door. The menu offers "Dead Chicken" and "Cheeseburgers . . . with cheese." Ask for a napkin and Juan or Robert will offer a handful of used ones. But things were not always so lighthearted. Robert says his father was a "very serious person, serious about everything." So serious that 10 years after opening the Snow Cap doctors told him he was overstressed and needed to relax or he wasn't going to be around for long. He lightened up by making his customers laugh. As he became more comfortable in that role, the high jinks became a staple. Not to give away all of Delgadillo's material, but beware of the yellow mustard bottle.

PEACH SPRINGS
c. 1935

Peach Springs is located at the southern tip of the 1-million-acre Hualapai (pronounced *wall-a-pie*) Indian reservation and is home to their tribal headquarters. It was founded in the early 1880s when the Santa Fe Railway established a water station on the site and named it for the peach trees that grow at a nearby spring. It is said that Mormon missionaries planted the trees there while visiting the region in 1852. The onetime western terminus of the Santa Fe Railway located at Peach Springs included a roundhouse, Harvey House restaurant, and a stagecoach line that offered tours to the Grand Canyon beginning in the 1880s.

Prior to 1935, U.S. Highway 66 was a two-lane dirt road through the center of town flanked by a couple of service stations and auto courts. The old tourist courts are long gone, but in their place stands the newly constructed Hualapai Lodge run by the Hualapai tribe. Many improvements were made to the section of road from Seligman through Peach Springs to Hackberry. On the eastern approach to Peach Springs, several of the original sections of Route 66 are visible parallel to the newer version of Route 66. In 1978, Interstate 40 construction on the 70-mile section from Seligman to Kingman was completed, bypassing many small towns along the way including Peach Springs, which was bypassed by 36 miles, the most of any town along the route.

KINGMAN
c. 1948

Kingman, located on the gently sloping Hualapai Valley between the Hualapai and Cerbat mountain ranges, began as a railroad siding near Beale's Springs along the newly constructed Atlantic & Pacific Railway. Originally known as Middleton, the name was changed to Kingman in 1882 for Lewis Kingman, a line surveyor on the railroad. The first train pulled into town on March 28, 1883, and Kingman, the little camp by the tracks, has been a major transportation hub for the western states ever since. Kingman flourished during the early 1900s, and many of the buildings constructed then survive today, including the old Brunswick Hotel opened in 1909. Arizona's first commercial airport, Port Kingman, was also opened there in 1929.

Being such an important transportation gateway, it's ironic that most Kingman streets, including Route 66 through town, remained unpaved until around 1940. Stranger still is the fact that until 1941, Kingman was surrounded by fencing to keep wandering livestock off the streets. Kingman has a few Hollywood connections, as well. Clark Gable and Carole Lombard were married at St. John's Methodist church in 1939, and well-known Hollywood entertainer Andy Devine was raised in Kingman; Front Street (Route 66) was changed to Andy Devine Avenue in 1955. In 1953 Interstate 40 was completed in the area, making Kingman one of the first Mother Road cities to be bypassed.

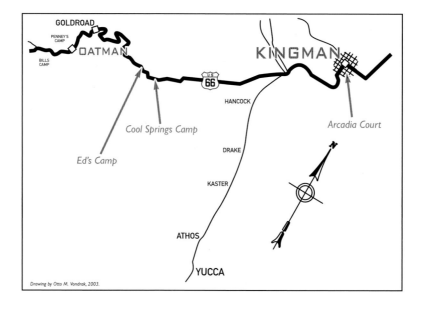

Drawing by Otto M. Vondrak, 2003.

ARCADIA COURT, KINGMAN
c. 1938

In its heyday the Arcadia Court catered to the "well to do." The back of this post card advertises, "Quiet and restful. Luxurious furnishings and the finest appointments for the fastidious guest. Healthiest climate (no humidity) and purest water. Special quarters for chauffeurs and maids." Eventually owners eliminated the garages to make way for more sleeping rooms, and during the early 1950s the Arcadia was remodeled and expanded to include 48 rooms. A heated swimming pool was also added later to keep up with the growing demands of the traveling public. After the Interstates bypassed their towns, many of the historic auto courts along Route 66 began a slow decline. The Arcadia Court was no exception. As motorists blew by

Kingman on I-40, the Arcadia Lodge, as it is now known, was left in the dust. Eventually, the classic auto court fell into a state of disrepair and local undesirables began calling the court home. Police were frequent visitors and the fine reputation the Arcadia Court once enjoyed became a distant memory. After a string of disinterested owners, the property was once again sold in 2001. Current managers Frank and Susan Brace are in the process of remodeling all the rooms. The drug dealers and prostitutes are long gone and with the help of the new owner, the Braces hope to once again make the Arcadia a stop of choice for the "fastidious guest."

COOL SPRINGS CAMP, WEST OF KINGMAN
c. 1939

N. R. Dunton built the Cool Springs Camp in the Black Mountains on the approach to Sitgreaves Pass in 1927. Being the resourceful person he was, he constructed the original buildings entirely out of stones gathered along the highway. In June 1936 Dunton sold the property to James and Mary Walker from Indiana. The Walker family, including their four children, moved to Cool Springs that summer and in January 1937 remodeled the business, adding a restaurant and bar. Mary divorced James after a few years and remarried a gentleman named Floyd Spidell, who added a full-service garage and guest cabins, turning the camp into a fully appointed travel stop. Eventually Mary and Floyd divorced and the business was left to Floyd.

The Cool Springs Camp was a very popular destination among travelers, as well as nearby Kingman residents. Well known for its fabulous chicken dinners, "locals" commuted as far as 20 miles to dine on the famous fowl. The Interstate bypassed this dangerous section of Highway 66 in the Black Mountains in 1952 in favor of a straighter and safer route to Topock, Arizona. After the realignment, business slowed to a crawl and the Cool Springs Camp was permanently shut down in 1964 when Floyd packed up and moved to Kingman. Ned Leuchtner of Kenilworth, Illinois, recently purchased the Cool Springs Camp site and at this writing was rebuilding the stone gas station.

COOLEST
SPOT
ON THE
DESERT

21 miles west
of Kingman,
9 miles east
of Oatman
ARIZONA
on U. S. Hwy. 66

E3910

ED'S CAMP, EAST OF GOLDROAD
c. 1947

Beginning the rugged approach to Sitgreaves Pass from the east, one of the most feared and dreaded sections on all of Route 66, travelers will notice the fading letters of Ed's Camp, spelled out in painted white rocks on the side of a hill. Lowell "Ed" Edgerton purchased the property that Ed's Camp sits on in the late 1930s, hoping to cash in on the ever-increasing flow of tourists. Throughout the 1930s and 1940s, Edgerton expanded his desert oasis to include a grocery store, gas station, trailer camp, and souvenir shop. It was a "camp" in every sense of the word—there were never any cabins or rooms at the site. Motorists on a budget would pull in and sleep in tents or in their cars. For $1, a tired traveler with a little bit of extra cash could sleep on a cot in a screened porch. Water was an-all-too precious commodity and was sold to guests on a per-bucket basis unless they paid the buck to spend the night—then it was free.

Edgerton went on to become a world-renowned figure in the field of geology. Amateur geologists came from around the world to hunt the area for precious stones, paying Edgerton a small fee for the privilege. In 1952, Route 66 was realigned around the Black Mountains from Kingman to Topock, bypassing the steep and treacherous mountain pass. Ed died in 1978, but his camp remains, for all intents and purposes undisturbed and hearkening back to better days.

OATMAN
c. 1929

Oatman, originally Vivian, sprang up from the blistering Mojave Desert when gold was discovered in 1902. After major gold strikes in 1908 and 1913, the population rose to as many as 10,000. By 1916 it was a bustling, thriving community. By the 1930s, gold strikes were few and mining operations began to diminish. As World War II wound up, the federal government ordered the remainder of the open mines closed, arguing the manpower was needed elsewhere. Thankfully, Route 66 ran directly through the center of town and the burgeoning tourist trade helped the community survive.

When 66 was rerouted in 1952, the Kingman *Daily Miner* reported, "One afternoon in 1952 traffic was coming steadily over Sitgreaves Pass, then it was silent. Someone rushed to Oatman with the news that they had cut the ribbon on the new section of U.S. Highway 66 between Kingman and Topock. Six of the seven service station families started to leave town the following day and owners of other businesses followed." After the bypass Oatman's population sank to a low of 60. The burros that worked in the mines were left behind. Their wild descendents wander Oatman's main street, looking for handouts and serving as one of the popular tourist attractions in Oatman. Another popular spot is the Oatman Hotel, where Clark Gable and Carole Lombard spent their honeymoon night. The room has been preserved and kept in its original state.

OATMAN, ARIZONA

CALIFORNIA

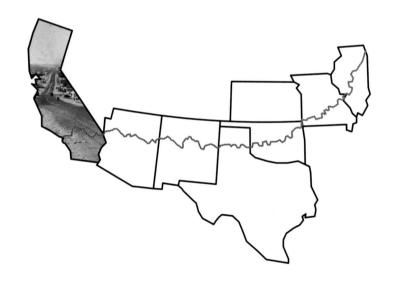

In the 1930s, countless Dust Bowl families left the drought-plagued heartland in search of a better life. The Great Depression was also in full swing and Route 66 to California was the escape route of choice. These early travelers who braved Sitgreaves Pass and perilous sections in Arizona must have first been disappointed in their destination. After crossing the Colorado River, expecting a glimpse of rich and fertile land filled with blossoming orange groves, they found more desert.

The first town after crossing the Colorado was Needles, where summer temperatures can soar to 125 degrees Fahrenheit. Imagine piling all your worldly possessions on an old Ford, tires barely keeping the rims from grinding on pavement, leaving all you knew behind, and suffering incredible heat and hardships, only to find more of what you just left behind. The Mojave Desert between Needles and Barstow, 150 blistering miles via the early alignment, was some of the most treacherous road on all of Route 66. Tiny hamlets along this stretch provided motorists with not much more than the essentials. Throughout Route 66's history, wrecker services along this section worked 24 hours a day, picking up stranded motorists or towing the really unlucky ones involved in accidents. During World War II the region was used by Patton to train his troops for battle against the Germans in North Africa.

Veterans of this blistering stretch of Route 66 knew to travel by night and to carry plenty of water. Once they reached Barstow, most Dust Bowl families left the Mother Road and headed north toward Bakersfield, hoping to find work in the farmlands of the San Joaquin Valley. Travel from Barstow to Los Angeles was relatively worry-free compared to the desert crossing, but not without its own perils. The Cajon Pass, "Gateway to Southern California," posed a formidable challenge as it wound its way down a difficult grade to San Bernardino. From there, 66 sliced through Upland, Azusa, Duarte, Arcadia, and Pasadena. The original western terminus of Route 66 was the intersection of Broadway and 7th Street in downtown Los Angeles. On January 1, 1936, the route was extended through Hollywood to Santa Monica, where it took a left-hand turn on to Lincoln Boulevard and ended at the intersection with Olympic Boulevard. Contrary to popular belief, Route 66 never reached the Santa Monica Pier or the Pacific Ocean.

Los Angeles saw so many alignment changes over the years that a complete guidebook, *Route 66 in Los Angeles County* by Scott R Piotrowski, was dedicated to unraveling its mysteries. One notable realignment, the Arroyo Seco Parkway, was considered the first freeway west of the Mississippi. Construction was completed on the Parkway in the late 1940s, and it is listed as a National Scenic Byway.

Whether you were a migrant family fleeing the Dust Bowl, an unemployed factory worker looking for a better life during the Great Depression, an actor dreaming of making it big in Hollywood, or simply taking the family on its annual summer vacation, reaching California was the collective dream and U.S. Highway 66 was the bright beacon that helped guide the masses and transform those dreams into reality.

NEEDLES
c. 1929

The town of Needles was established in 1883 as a burgeoning railroad town and mining hub. To this day the railroad is by far its largest employer. Known as "The Gateway to California," Needles got its name from the jagged, sharply pointed peaks of the Black Mountains southwest of the town. To say that it gets hot in this part of the country is a major understatement. Jack Rittenhouse, author of 1946's *A Guide Book to Highway 66:* "In the hot months, it is advisable to make the drive from Needles to Barstow, over the Mojave Desert, either in the evening, night or early morning hours. In any case, it is advisable to carry extra water for the car."

Needles is home to the ornate El Garces, a onetime Harvey House that served railroad customers until 1949. Today, the Friends of El Garces hope to restore the magnificent structure for future generations to enjoy. In 1973 Interstate 40 was completed and tourist traffic fell dramatically as cars disappeared. A few of the classic motels and cafés survive, but that's a relative term. In this part of the country, Route 66 was born out of crude dirt pathways and wooden-plank roads that twisted their way across the desert. The onetime concrete artery that fed life into the western part of our nation is slowly and begrudgingly returning to that desert, as America's Main Street begins its gradual decay and the Mojave slowly reclaims its own.

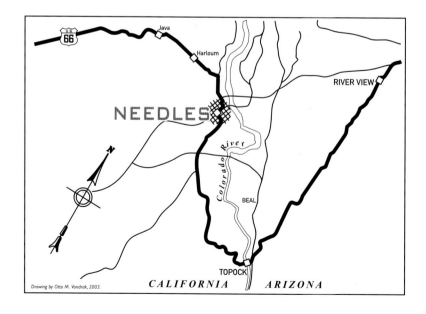

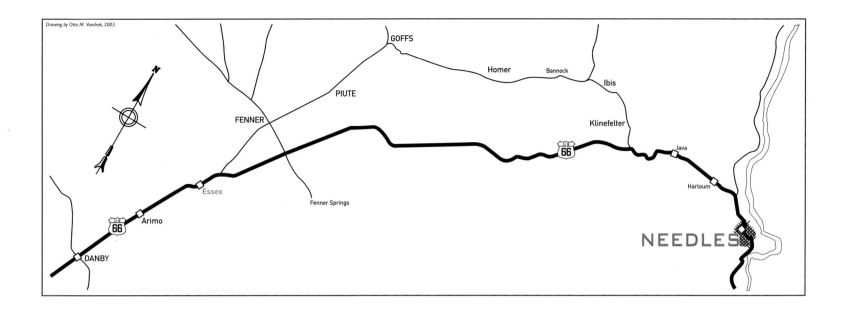

Drawing by Otto M. Vondrak, 2003.

ESSEX
c. 1942

It is rumored that the tiny Mojave Desert town of Essex was founded when an unlucky motorist broke down in the area. With no towing or service station for miles, he decided to stay and call this desert spot home. Being an enterprising sort, he opened a towing service with a café, and Essex was born, located on a section of road originally known as the National Old Trails Highway. In 1926 this road was redesignated U.S. Highway 66. During the late 1940s and the 1950s, Essex offered travelers and tourists all the essentials needed for desert travel, including towing services, gasoline, food, and water. Back in the days when tourist traffic regularly flowed through town, clean water was a precious commodity sold to

motorists at 10 cents per glass for drinking; unfiltered water was sold at 10 cents per gallon for car radiators. The Automobile Club of Southern California graciously installed a free drinking fountain in town, alleviating the outrageous charges levied by local businesses. This stone well-like structure still stands a couple of hundred feet from the onetime market and just a few feet south of the highway. Although no longer in service, it reminds us of the dangers that once confronted early motorists traveling the Mojave. The U.S. Postal Service is the only remaining Essex business still in operation. The café was reopened sometime in the 1990s but was eventually shut down and remains abandoned.

CADIZ SUMMIT SERVICE, CADIZ
c. 1946

Cadiz Summit Service was originally built in the 1920s by George and Minnie Tienken on the old alignment of U.S. Highway 66 that ran through Goffs and Fenner, California. In 1931, Route 66 was realigned from Goffs to create a straighter, more direct path. Undaunted, George and Minnie moved the business, buildings and all, to this new location about 18 miles west of Essex. After a long, hot, and often hazardous summer day's travel in the Mojave, this lonely California rest stop must have been a very welcome site. Standing in the now-deserted parking area, one can almost see and hear the hustle and bustle of hot and thirsty travelers looking for a cold drink or a quick snack.

Interstate 40 bypassed this section of Route 66 in 1972, cutting off its lifeblood and allowing another landmark roadside business to fall victim to the name of progress. Soon after the bypass, traffic along the route slowed to a trickle and Cadiz Summit closed its doors. In no time, vandals and looters took over and a fire finally destroyed what was left. Jack Rittenhouse, in his *Guide Book to Highway 66,* wrote of Cadiz Summit, "a handful of tourist cabins, a café and gas station comprise this desert oasis." No visible evidence of the cabins remains.

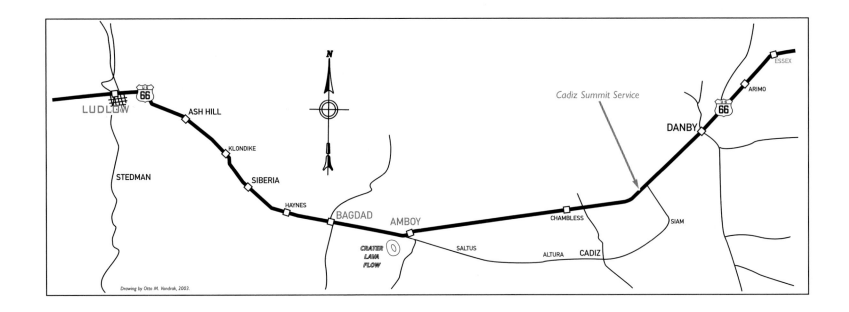

Drawing by Otto M. Vondrak, 2003.

HIGHWAY "66" AMBOY, CALIF. 344

AMBOY
c. 1946

Both Herman "Buster" Burris and Roy Crowl figure prominently in Amboy's growth during the glory days of Route 66. A native Texan, Burris was working as a mechanic at the nearby March Air Base when he met and married Crowl's daughter. He and Crowl went on to become business partners. In 1940 Burris opened a repair shop and in 1945 a café. A couple of cabins were also built to accommodate customers waiting for repairs. In 1948 he began construction on a motel that was completed in its present form in 1952. The famous "Roy's Motel" sign was built in 1959 and remains one of the most recognizable structures on all of Route 66.

"I used to think everybody in the world was driving through Amboy," said Burris. The town's population grew at a frantic pace as mechanics, waitresses, and motel help moved to the area. When Interstate 40 bypassed Amboy in the 1970s, "It was just like somebody put up a gate across Route 66. The traffic just plain stopped," recalled Burris. Through the years Burris expanded the business as opportunities arose, until one day he found he owned the whole town. In the early 1980s he put the complete town up for sale. The asking price: $350,000. Walt Wilson and Timothy White purchased Amboy in 2000 and rented the town out as a film location. In 2002 Amboy was once again put up for sale, this time on eBay, but the reserve price was not met and Amboy remains unsold.

BAGDAD
c. 1950s

The desert town of Bagdad began in 1883 as a small railroad stop. When the Orange Blossom and Lady Lou mines struck pay dirt around the turn of the century, the town of Bagdad became a major gold shipping point. As the mining industry declined, so did Bagdad's fortunes. In 1923 the town lost its post office and by 1937 the mines were closing at a rapid pace, but the Santa Fe depot remained to transport ore, and Bagdad continued to be a coal and water stop for steam engines.

By the 1940s most of the mines were closed and Bagdad, whose population once peaked at close to 600, dropped to about 20. Still, business from Route 66 traffic kept some of the town alive. Paul Limon, a onetime gas station attendant remembers, "Bagdad was a lively little place. People from all over the desert would come here because of the Bagdad Café, owned and operated by a woman named Alice Lawrence. The Bagdad Café was the only place for miles around with a dance floor and jukebox." The café, gas station, cabins, and market continued to serve travelers until 1972, when the Interstate opened to the north. The 1988 film *Bagdad Café,* inspired by the town and its café, was actually filmed in Newberry Springs, 50 miles west of Bagdad. In 1991 the site was used as storage for a natural gas project and the town was wiped clean. Today, there is no evidence the town ever existed.

LUDLOW
c. 1940

"In comparison with neighboring towns, Ludlow is a metropolis," read the 1939 WPA guide to U.S. Highway 66 in California. The population of Ludlow, including railroad crews' families and miners who worked the nearby Bagdad Chase Mines, reached a peak of about 150. Established in 1882, the town was named for William B. Ludlow, who repaired railcars for the nearby Santa Fe Railway. This area of the Mojave was so isolated that the Santa Fe had to import water in tanker cars. The water was then pumped into an elevated storage tank and gravity fed to Ludlow's thirsty residents until 1965 when Ludlow's first

well was dug. The Murphy Brothers Mercantile Store was the most prominent business, along with a "mall" consisting of a pool hall/tavern, grocery store, and restaurant that served locals and travelers alike. When Route 66 was the main artery to the West, Ludlow enjoyed a booming travel business. That ended when Interstate 40 bypassed the town in 1972, marking Ludlow's second economic collapse, the first being the decline of mining in the 1940s. Today, Ludlow consists of a couple of service stations, a café, and a motel to serve the needs of Interstate travelers and Route 66 explorers.

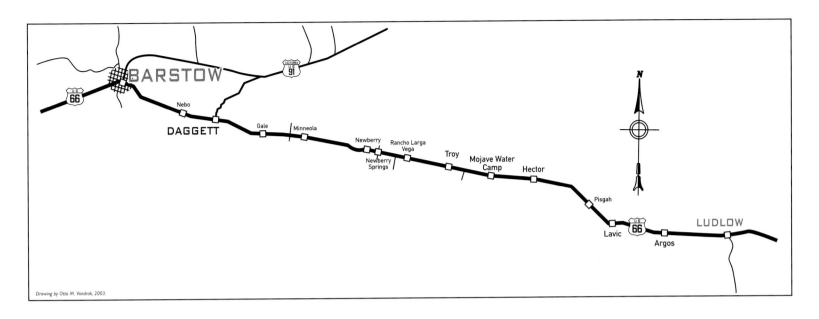

Drawing by Otto M. Vondrak, 2003.

BARSTOW
c. 1948

More than 150 miles of harsh, sun-baked terrain awaited motorists departing Needles for Barstow. Previously known as Waterman, the town's name was changed in 1886 to honor Santa Fe President William Barstow Strong after that railroad built a depot in town. (His middle name was used because Kansas already had a "Strong" station on the line.) A new railroad depot, Casa del Desierto, completed in 1911, was added to the National Register of Historic Places in 1975. Today, the beautifully restored "House in the Desert" is home to the Route 66 Mother Road Museum (www.Barstow66museum.itgo.com).

During Barstow's early years the town was located on the north side of the railroad tracks but as a result of frequent expansion of the railroad, was eventually relocated to the south. Four-lane Interstate 15 was completed from Barstow to Victorville in 1958, shortening the distance between the two towns by 5 miles. The bypass, as elsewhere, had a tremendous negative impact on Barstow's downtown business district, but the city found new life at its eastern edge. There, the intersection of Interstate 40 and Interstate 15 functions as an ideal refueling point and rest stop.

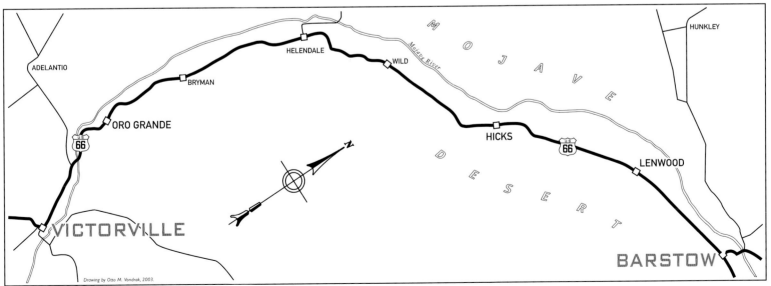

VICTORVILLE
c. 1939

The small town of Victorville is located 97 miles northeast of Los Angeles at the western edge of the Mojave Desert. In 1885, the Southern California Railroad built a station there and the area became known as Huntington Station. It was later dubbed "Victor" after the railroad's construction superintendent, Jacob Nash Victor, then renamed Victorville when the mail service began confusing Victor, California, with Victor, Colorado. Victorville, a favorite location for filming western "B movies" in the 1960s, has survived and grown since the Interstate totally bypassed the town in 1972, as is evidenced by the population increase from 11,200 in 1972 to 71,224 today. At the time the above postcard photograph was taken, the city's population was listed as approximately 2,500.

Route 66 ran west through Victorville on D Street, making a right turn onto 7th Street, and continuing through town toward the steep grade of the Cajon Pass on its way to San Bernardino before terminating in Los Angeles. The popular California Route 66 Museum (www.califrt66museum.org) is located on Route 66 in "Old Town" Victorville and is housed in the onetime Red Rooster Café building, where the *Jazz Singer,* starring Neil Diamond, was filmed.

SOURCES

Books

Curtis, C. H. *The Missouri US 66 Tour Book.* St. Louis, Mo.: D. I. Enterprises, 1994.

Noe, Sally. *66 Sights on Route 66.* Gallup, N.Mex.: Gallup Downtown Development Group, 1992.

Piotrowski, Scott. *Finding the End of the Mother Road.* Pasadena, Calif.: 66 Productions, 2003.

Rittenhouse, Jack D. *A Guide Book to Highway 66.* Albuquerque, N.Mex.: (Reprint of 1946 printing) Univ. of New Mexico Press, 1989.

Ross, Jim. *Oklahoma Route 66.* Arcadia, Okla. Ghost Town Press, 2001.

Schneider, Jill. *Route 66 Across New Mexico: A Wanderer's Guide.* Albuquerque, N.Mex.: Univ. of New Mexico Press, 1991.

Scott, Quinta and Susan Croce Kelly. Route 66: *The Highway and Its People.* Norman, Okla.: Univ. of Oklahoma Press, 1988.

————. *Along Route 66.* Norman, Okla.: Univ. of Oklahoma Press, 2000.

Snyder, Tom. *The Route 66 Traveler's Companion.* New York: St. Martin's Press, 1990.

Teague, Thomas. *Searching for 66.* Springfield, Ill.: Samizdat House, 1991.

Wallis, Michael. *Route 66: The Mother Road.* New York: St. Martin's Press, 1990.

Weis, John. *Traveling the New, Historic Route 66 of Illinois.* Frankfort, Ill.: A. O. Motivation Programs, 1997.

Witzel, Michael. *Route 66 Remembered.* Osceola, Wis.: Motorbooks International, 1996.

Periodicals

National Historic Route 66 Federation News (www.national66.org), 1995–present.

Route 66 Magazine (www.route66magazine.com), 1993–present.

Wallace, Norman. "The Scenic Wonderland Highway." *Arizona Highways* May 1955

Interviews

Adam, Nick. Ariston Café, Litchfield, Ill.

Alderson, Jace. Sands Motel, Moriarty, N.Mex.

Berger, Lois. Log Cabin Lodge, Gallup, N.Mex.

Brace, Frank and Susan. Arcadia Lodge, Kingman, Ariz.

Delgadillo, Robert. Snow Cap, Seligman, Ariz.

Edmunds, Dub. Jesse's Café/MidPoint Café, Adrian, Tex.

Edwards, Ernie. Ernie's Pig Hip, Broadwell, Ill.

Ferguson, John. Boots Motel, Carthage, Mo.

Goodridge, Edward. Vernelle's Motel, Newburg, Mo.

Hauser, Fran. MidPoint Café, Adrian, Tex.

Kraft, Bob. The Riviera, Gardner, Ill.

Lehman, Ramona. Munger-Moss Motel, Lebanon, Mo.

Manker, Gina. Log Cabin Inn, Pontiac, Ill.

Miller, Atholl "Jiggs". Devils Elbow, Mo.

Mudd, Roy. Wagon Wheel Motel, Cuba, Mo.

Murphy, Lorie. Shady Rest Court, West Tulsa, Okla.

Natha, Mohamed. Aztec Motel, Albuquerque, N.Mex.

Noe, Sally. Thoreau, N.Mex.

Pendya, Mr. Rest Haven Motor Court, Springfield, Mo.

Radosevich, John. Johnnie's Café, Thoreau, N.Mex.

Roberts, Teresa. Pioneer Motel, Springfield, Ill.

Sanchez Jr., Canuto. Lakeview Courts, Santa Rosa, N.Mex.

Stevens, Les. Steve's Café, Chenoa, Ill.

Vidas, Zora. Wishing Well Motel, LaGrange, Ill.

Waldmire, Sue. Cozy Dog, Springfield, Ill.

Werth, Wilfred. Redwood Motel, Lincoln, Ill.

Whaley, Tresa. Vega Motel, Vega, Tex.

INDEX